Your Personal Horoscope 2015

Aries

Your Personal Horoscope 2015

Aries

21st March–20th April

igloobooks

Published in 2014
by Igloo Books Ltd

Cottage Farm
Sywell
NN6 0BJ
www.igloobooks.com

Produced for Igloo Books by W. Foulsham & Co. Ltd, The Old Barrel Store, Drayman's Lane, Marlow, Bucks SL7 2FF, England

HUN001 0714
2 4 6 8 10 9 7 5 3 1
ISBN: 978-1-783-43637-8

This is an abridged version of material originally published in Old Moore's Horoscope and Astral Diary.

Printed and manufactured in China

CONTENTS

INTRODUCTION

Your Personal Horoscopes have been specifically created to allow you to get the most from astrological patterns and the way they have a bearing on not only your zodiac sign, but nuances within it. Using the diary section of the book you can read about the influences and possibilities of each and every day of the year. It will be possible for you to see when you are likely to be cheerful and happy or those times when your nature is in retreat and you will be more circumspect. The diary will help to give you a feel for the specific 'cycles' of astrology and the way they can subtly change your day-to-day life. For example, when you see the sign ☿, this means that the planet Mercury is retrograde at that time. Retrograde means it appears to be running backwards through the zodiac. Such a happening has a significant effect on communication skills, but this is only one small aspect of how the Personal Horoscope can help you.

With Your Personal Horoscope the story doesn't end with the diary pages. It includes simple ways for you to work out the zodiac sign the Moon occupied at the time of your birth, and what this means for your personality. In addition, if you know the time of day you were born, it is possible to discover your Ascendant, yet another important guide to your personal make-up and potential.

Many readers are interested in relationships and in knowing how well they get on with people of other astrological signs. You might also be interested in the way you appear to very different sorts of individuals. If you are such a person, the section on Venus will be of particular interest. Despite the rapidly changing position of this planet, you can work out your Venus sign, and learn what bearing it will have on your life.

Using Your Personal Horoscope you can travel on one of the most fascinating and rewarding journeys that anyone can take – the journey to a better realisation of self.

THE ESSENCE OF ARIES

Exploring the Personality of Aries the Ram

(21ST MARCH – 20TH APRIL)

What's in a sign?

Aries is not the first sign of the zodiac by accident. It's the place in the year when the spring begins, and so it represents some of the most dynamic forces in nature, and within the zodiac as a whole. As a result the very essence of your nature is geared towards promoting yourself in life and pushing your ideas forward very positively. You don't brook a great deal of interference in your life, but you are quite willing to help others as much as you can, provided that to do so doesn't curb your natural desire to get on in life.

Aries people are not universally liked, though your true friends remain loyal to you under almost any circumstances. But why should it be that such a dynamic and go-getting person does meet with some opposition? The answer is simple: not everyone is quite so sure of themselves as you are and many tend to get nervous when faced with the sheer power of the Aries personality. If there is one factor within your own control that could counter these problems it is the adoption of some humility – that commodity which is so important for you to dredge from the depths of your nature. If you only show the world that you are human, and that you are well aware of the fact, most people would follow you willingly to the very gates of hell. The most successful Aries subjects know this fact and cultivate it to the full.

Your executive skills are never in doubt and you can get almost anything practical done whilst others are still jumping from foot to foot. That's why you are such a good organiser and are so likely to be out there at the front of any venture. Adventurous and quite willing to show your bravery in public, you can even surprise yourself sometimes with the limits you are likely to go to in order to reach solutions that seem right to you.

Kind to those you take to, you can be universally loved when working at your best. Despite this there will be times in your life when you simply can't understand why some people just don't like you. Maybe there's an element of jealousy involved.

Aries resources

The part of the zodiac occupied by the sign of Aries has, for many centuries, been recognised as the home of self-awareness. This means that there isn't a person anywhere else in the zodiac that has a better knowledge of self than you do. But this isn't necessarily an intellectual process with Aries, more a response to the very blood that is coursing through your veins. Aries' success doesn't so much come from spending hours working out the pros and cons of any given course of action, more from the thrill of actually getting stuck in. If you find yourself forced into a life that means constantly having to think everything through to the tiniest detail, there is likely to be some frustration in evidence.

Aries is ruled by Mars, arguably the most go-getting of all the planets in the solar system. Mars is martial and demands practical ways of expressing latent power. It also requires absolute obedience from subordinates. When this is forthcoming, Aries individuals are the most magnanimous people to be found anywhere. Loyalty is not a problem and there have been many instances in history when Aries people were quite willing to die for their friends if necessary.

When other people are willing to give up and go with the flow, you will still be out there pitching for the result that seems most advantageous to you. It isn't something you can particularly control and those who don't know you well could find you sometimes curt and over-demanding as a result. But because you are tenacious you can pick the bones out of any situation and will usually arrive at your desired destination, if you don't collapse with fatigue on the way.

Routines, or having to take life at the pace of less motivated types, won't suit you at all. Imprisonment of any sort, even in a failed relationship, is sheer torture and you will move heaven and earth to get out into the big, wide world, where you can exploit your natural potential to the full. Few people know you really well because you don't always explain yourself adequately. The ones who do adore you.

Beneath the surface

Whereas some zodiac signs are likely to spend a great deal of their lives looking carefully at the innermost recesses of their own minds, Aries individuals tend to prefer the cut and thrust of the practical world. Aries people are not natural philosophers, but that doesn't mean that you aren't just as complicated beneath the surface as any of your astrological brothers and sisters. So what is it that makes the Aries firebrand think and act in the way that it does? To a great extent it is a lack of basic self-confidence.

This statement might seem rather odd, bearing in mind that a fair percentage of the people running our world were born under the sign of the Ram, but it is true nevertheless. Why? Because people who know themselves and their capabilities really well don't feel the constant need to prove themselves in the way that is the driving force of your zodiac sign. Not that your naturally progressive tendencies are a fault. On the contrary, if used correctly they can help you to create a much better, fairer and happier world, at least in your own vicinity.

The fact that you occasionally take your ball and go home if you can't get your own way is really down to the same insecurity that is noticeable through many facets of your nature. If Aries can't rule, it often doesn't want to play at all. A deep resentment and a brooding quality can build up in the minds and souls of some thwarted Aries types, a tendency that you need to combat. Better by far to try and compromise, itself a word that doesn't exist in the vocabularies of the least enlightened people born under the sign of the Ram. Once this lesson is learned, inner happiness increases and you relax into your life much more.

The way you think about others is directly related to the way you consider they think about you. This leads to another surprising fact regarding the zodiac sign. Aries people absolutely hate to be disliked, though they would move heaven and earth to prove that this isn't the case. And as a result Aries both loves and hates with a passion. Deep inside you can sometimes be a child shivering in the dark. If you only realise this fact your path to happiness and success is almost assured. Of course to do so takes a good deal of courage – but that's a commodity you don't lack.

Making the best of yourself

It would be quite clear to any observer that you are not the sort of person who likes to hang around at the back of a queue, or who would relish constantly taking orders from people who may not know situations as well as you do. For that reason alone you are better in positions that see you out there at the front, giving commands and enjoying the cut and thrust of everyday life. In a career sense this means that whatever you do you are happiest telling those around you how to do it too. Many Aries people quite naturally find their way to the top of the tree and don't usually have too much trouble staying there.

It is important to remember, however, that there is another side to your nature: the giving qualities beneath your natural dominance. You can always be around when people need you the most, encouraging and even gently pushing when it is necessary. By keeping friends and being willing to nurture relationships across a broad spectrum, you gradually get to know what makes those around you tick. This makes for a more patient and understanding sort of Aries subject – the most potent of all.

Even your resilience is not endless, which is why it is important to remember that there are times when you need rest. Bearing in mind that you are not superhuman is the hardest lesson to learn, but the admission brings humility, something that Aries needs to cultivate whenever possible.

Try to avoid living a restricted life and make your social contacts frequent and important. Realise that there is much more to life than work and spend some of your free time genuinely attempting to help those who are less well off than you are. Crucially you must remember that 'help' is not the same as domination.

The impressions you give

This section may well be of less interest to Aries subjects than it would be to certain other zodiac signs. The reason is quite clear. Aries people are far less interested in what others think about them than almost anyone else – or at least they tell themselves that they are. Either way it is counterproductive to ignore the opinions of the world at large because to do so creates stumbling blocks, even in a practical sense.

Those around you probably find you extremely capable and well able to deal with almost any situation that comes your way. Most are willing to rely heavily on you and the majority would almost instinctively see you as a leader. Whether or not they like you at the same time is really dependent on the way you handle situations. That's the difference between the go-getting, sometimes selfish type of Aries subject and the more enlightened amongst this illustrious sign.

You are viewed as being exciting and well able to raise enthusiasm for almost any project that takes your fancy. Of course this implies a great responsibility because you are always expected to come up with the goods. The world tends to put certain people on a pedestal, and you are one of them. On the other side of the coin we are all inclined to fire arrows at the elevated, so maintaining your position isn't very easy.

Most of the time you are seen as being magnanimous and kind, factors that you can exploit, whilst at the same time recognising the depth of the responsibility that comes with being an Aries subject. It might not be a bad thing to allow those around you to see that you too have feet of clay. This will make them respect and support you all the more, and even Aries people really do need to feel loved. A well-balanced Aries subject is one of the most elevated spirits to be found anywhere.

The way forward

You certainly enjoy life more when looking at it from the top of the tree. Struggling to get by is not in the least interesting to your zodiac sign and you can soon become miserable if things are not going well for you. That's why it is probably quite justified in your case to work tenaciously in order to achieve your objectives. Ideally, once you have realised some sort of success and security for yourself, you should then be willing to sit and watch life go by a little more. In fact this doesn't happen. The reason for this is clear. The Aries subject who learns how to succeed rarely knows when to stop – it's as simple as that.

Splitting your life into different components can help, if only because this means that you don't get the various elements mixed up. So, for example, don't confuse your love life with your professional needs, or your family with colleagues. This process allows you to view life in manageable chunks and also makes it possible for you to realise when any one of them may be working well. As a result you will put the effort where it's needed, and enjoy what is going well for you.

If you want to know real happiness you will also have to learn that acquisition for its own sake brings hollow rewards at best. When your talents are being turned outward to the world at large, you are one of the most potent and successful people around. What is more you should find yourself to be a much happier person when you are lending a hand to the wider world. This is possible, maybe outside of your normal professional sphere, though even where voluntary work is concerned it is important not to push yourself to the point of fatigue.

Keep yourself physically fit, without necessarily expecting that you can run to the South Pole and back, and stay away from too many stimulants, such as alcohol and nicotine. The fact is that you are best when living a healthy life, but it doesn't help either if you make even abstinence into an art form. Balance is important, as is moderation – itself a word that is difficult for you to understand. In terms of your approach to other people it's important to realise that everyone has a specific point of view. These might be different to yours, but they are not necessarily wrong. Sort out the friends who are most important to you and stick with them, whilst at the same time realising that almost everyone can be a pal – with just a little effort.

ARIES ON THE CUSP

Astrological profiles are altered for those people born at either the beginning or the end of a zodiac sign, or, more properly, on the cusps of a sign. In the case of Aries this would be on the 21st of March and for two or three days after, and similarly at the end of the sign, probably from the 18th to the 20th of April.

The Pisces Cusp – March 21st to March 24th

With the Sun so close to the zodiac sign of Pisces at the time you were born, it is distinctly possible that you have always had some doubts when reading a character breakdown written specifically for the sign of Aries. This isn't surprising because no zodiac sign has a definite start or end, they merely merge together. As a result there are some of the characteristics of the sign of the Fishes that are intermingled with the qualities of Aries in your nature.

What we probably find, as a result, is a greater degree of emotional sensitivity and a tendency to be more cognisant of what the rest of humanity is feeling. This is not to imply that Aries is unfeeling, but rather that Pisceans actively make humanity their business.

You are still able to achieve your most desired objectives in the practical world, but on the way, you stop to listen to the heartbeat of the planet on which you live. A very good thing, of course, but at the same time there is some conflict created if your slightly dream-like tendencies get in the way of your absolute need to see things through to their logical conclusion.

Nobody knows you better than you know yourself, or at least that's what the Aries qualities within you say, but that isn't always verified by some of the self-doubt that comes from the direction of the Fishes. As in all matters astrological, a position of balance has to be achieved in order to reconcile the differing qualities of your nature. In your case, this is best accomplished by being willing to stop and think once in a while and by refusing to allow your depth to be a problem.

Dealt with properly, the conjoining of Pisces and Aries can be a wondrous and joyful affair, a harmony of opposites that always makes you interesting to know. Your position in the world is naturally one of authority but at the same time you need to serve. That's why some people with this sort of mixture of astrological qualities would make such good administrators in a hospital, or in any position where the alternate astrological needs are well balanced. In the chocolate box of life you are certainly a 'soft centre'.

The Taurus Cusp – April 18th to April 20th

The merge from Aries to Taurus is much less well defined than the one at the other side of Aries, but it can be very useful to you all the same. Like the Pisces-influenced Aries you may be slightly more quiet than would be the case with the Ram taken alone and your thought processes are probably not quite as fast. But to compensate for this fact you don't rush into things quite as much and are willing to allow ideas to mature more fully.

Your sense of harmony and beauty is strong and you know, in a very definite way, exactly what you want. As a result your home will be distinctive but tasteful and it's a place where you need space to be alone sometimes, which the true Aries subject probably does not. You do not lack the confidence to make things look the way you want them, but you have a need to display these things to the world at large and sometimes even to talk about how good you are at decoration and design.

If anyone finds you pushy, it is probably because they don't really know what makes you tick. Although you are willing to mix with almost anyone, you are more inclined, at base, to have a few very close friends who stay at the forefront of your life for a long time. It is likely that you enjoy refined company and you wouldn't take kindly to the dark, the sordid, or the downright crude in life.

Things don't get you down as much as can sometimes be seen to be the case for Taurus when taken alone and you are rarely stumped for a progressive and practical idea when one is needed most. At all levels, your creative energy is evident and some of you even have the ability to make this into a business, since Aries offers the practical and administrative spark that Taurus can sometimes lack.

In matters of love, you are ardent and sincere, probably an idealist, and you know what you want in a partner. Whilst this is also true in the case of Taurus, you are different, because you are much more likely, not only to look, but also to say something about the way you feel.

Being naturally friendly you rarely go short of the right sort of help and support when it is most vital. Part of the reason for this lies in the fact that you are so willing to be the sounding-board for the concerns of your friends. All in all you can be very contented with your lot, but you never stop searching for something better all the same. At its best, this is one of the most progressive cuspal matches of them all.

ARIES AND ITS ASCENDANTS

The nature of every individual on the planet is composed of the rich variety of zodiac signs and planetary positions that were present at the time of their birth. Your Sun sign, which in your case is Aries, is one of the many factors when it comes to assessing the unique person you are. Probably the most important consideration, other than your Sun sign, is to establish the zodiac sign that was rising over the eastern horizon at the time that you were born. This is your Ascending or Rising sign. Most popular astrology fails to take account of the Ascendant, and yet its importance remains with you from the very moment of your birth, through every day of your life. The Ascendant is evident in the way you approach the world, and so, when meeting a person for the first time, it is this astrological influence that you are most likely to notice first. Our Ascending sign essentially represents what we appear to be, while our Sun sign is what we feel inside ourselves.

The Ascendant also has the potential for modifying our overall nature. For example, if you were born at a time of day when Aries was passing over the eastern horizon (this would be around the time of dawn) then you would be classed as a double Aries. As such you would typify this zodiac sign, both internally and in your dealings with others. However, if your Ascendant sign turned out to be a Water sign, such as Pisces, there would be a profound alteration of nature, away from the expected qualities of Aries.

One of the reasons that popular astrology often ignores the Ascendant is that it has always been rather difficult to establish. We have found a way to make this possible by devising an easy-to-use table, which you will find on page 157 of this book. Using this, you can establish your Ascendant sign at a glance. You will need to know your rough time of birth, then it is simply a case of following the instructions.

For those readers who have no idea of their time of birth it might be worth allowing a good friend, or perhaps your partner, to read through the section that follows this introduction. Someone who deals with you on a regular basis may easily discover your Ascending sign, even though you could have some difficulty establishing it for yourself. A good understanding of this component of your nature is essential if you want to be aware of that 'other person' who is responsible for the way you make contact with the world at large. Your Sun sign, Ascendant sign, and the other pointers in this book

will, together, allow you a far better understanding of what makes you tick as an individual. Peeling back the different layers of your astrological make-up can be an enlightening experience, and the Ascendant may represent one of the most important layers of all.

Aries with Aries Ascendant

What you see is what you get with this combination. You typify the no-nonsense approach of Aries at its best. All the same this combination is quite daunting when viewed through the eyes of other, less dominant sorts of people. You tend to push your way though situations that would find others cowering in a corner and you are afraid of very little. With a determination to succeed that makes you a force to be reckoned with, you leave the world in no doubt as to your intentions and tend to be rather too brusque for your own good on occasions.

At heart you are kind and loving, able to offer assistance to the downtrodden and sad, and usually willing to take on board the cares of people who have a part to play in your life. No-one would doubt your sincerity, or your honesty, though you may utilise slightly less than orthodox ways of getting your own way on those occasions when you feel you have right on your side. You are a loving partner and a good parent, though where children are concerned you tend to be rather too protective. The trouble is that you know what a big, bad world it can be and probably feel that you are better equipped to deal with things than anyone else.

Aries with Taurus Ascendant

This is a much quieter combination, so much so that even experienced astrologers would be unlikely to recognise you as an Aries subject at all, unless of course they came to know you very well. Your approach to life tends to be quiet and considered and there is a great danger that you could suppress those feelings that others of your kind would be only too willing to verbalise. To compensate you are deeply creative and will think matters through much more readily than more dominant Aries types would be inclined to do. Reaching out towards the world, you are, nevertheless, somewhat locked inside yourself and can struggle to achieve the level of communication that you so desperately need. Frustration might easily follow, were it not for the fact that you possess a quiet determination that, to those in the know, is the clearest window through to your Aries soul.

The care for others is stronger here than with almost any other Aries type and you certainly demonstrate this at all levels. The fact is that you live a great percentage of your life in service to the people you take to, whilst at the same time being able to shut the door firmly in the face of people who irritate or anger you. You are deeply motivated towards family relationships.

Aries with Gemini Ascendant

A fairly jolly combination this, though by no means easy for others to come to terms with. You fly about from pillar to post and rarely stop long enough to take a breath. Admittedly this suits your own needs very well, but it can be a source of some disquiet to those around you, since they may not possess your energy or motivation. Those who know you well are deeply in awe of your capacity to keep going long after almost everyone else would have given up and gone home, though this quality is not always as wonderful as it sounds because it means that you put more pressure on your nervous system than just about any other astrological combination.

You need to be mindful of your nervous system, which responds to the erratic, mercurial quality of Gemini. Problems only really arise when the Aries part of you makes demands that the Gemini component finds difficult to deal with. There are paradoxes galore here and some of them need sorting out if you are ever fully to understand yourself, or are to be in a position when others know what makes you tick.

In relationships you might be a little fickle, but you are a real charmer and never stuck for the right words, no matter who you are dealing with. Your tenacity knows no bounds, though perhaps it should!

Aries with Cancer Ascendant

The main problem that you experience in life shows itself as a direct result of the meshing of these two very different zodiac signs. At heart Aries needs to dominate, whereas Cancer shows a desire to nurture. All too often the result can be a protective arm that is so strong that nobody could possibly get out from under it. Lighten your own load, and that of those you care for, by being willing to sit back and watch others please themselves a little. You might think that you know best, and your heart is clearly in the right place, but try to realise what life is like when someone is always on hand to tell you that they know better then you do.

But in a way this is a little severe, because you are fairly intuitive and your instincts would rarely lead you astray. Nobody could ask for a better partner or parent than you, though they might request a slightly less attentive one. In matters of work you are conscientious and are probably best suited to a job that means sorting out the kind of mess that humanity is so good at creating. You probably spend your spare time untangling balls of wool, though you are quite sporting too and could easily make the Olympics. Once there you would not win however, because you would be too concerned about all the other competitors.

Aries with Leo Ascendant

Here we come upon the first situation of Aries being allied with another Fire sign. This creates a character that could appear to be typically Aries at first sight and in many ways it is, though there are subtle differences that should not be ignored. Although you have the typical Aries ability to get things done, many of the tasks you do undertake will be for and on behalf of others. You can be proud, and on some occasions even haughty, and yet you are also regal in your bearing and honest to the point of absurdity. Nobody could doubt your sincerity and you have the soul of a poet combined with the courage of a lion.

All this is good, but it makes you rather difficult to approach, unless the person in question has first adopted a crouching and subservient attitude although you would not wish them to do so. It's simply that the impression you give and the motivation that underpins it are two quite different things. You are greatly respected and in the case of those individuals who know your real nature, you are also deeply loved. But life would be much simpler if you didn't always have to fight the wars that those around you are happy to start. Relaxation is a word that you don't really understand and you would do yourself a favour if you looked it up in a dictionary.

Aries with Virgo Ascendant

Virgo is steady and sure, though also fussy and stubborn. Aries is fast and determined, restless and active. It can already be seen that this is a rather strange meeting of characteristics and because Virgo is ruled by the capricious Mercury, the ultimate result will change from hour to hour and day to day. It isn't merely that others find it difficult to know where they are with you, they can't even understand what makes you tick. This will make you the subject of endless fascination and attention, at which you will be apparently surprised but inwardly pleased. If anyone ever really gets to know what goes on in that busy mind they may find the implications very difficult to deal with and it is a fact that only you would have the ability to live inside your crowded head.

As a partner and a parent you are second to none, though you tend to get on better with your children once they start to grow, since by this time you may be slightly less restricting to their own desires, which will often clash with your own on their behalf. You are capable of give and take and could certainly not be considered selfish, though your constant desire to get the best from everyone might occasionally be misconstrued.

Aries with Libra Ascendant

Libra has the tendency to bring out the best in any zodiac sign, and this is no exception when it comes together with Aries. You may, in fact, be the most comfortable of all Aries types, simply because Libra tempers some of your more assertive qualities and gives you the chance to balance out opposing forces, both inside yourself and in the world outside. You are fun to be with and make the staunchest friend possible. Although you are generally affable, few people would try to put one over on you, because they would quickly come to know how far you are willing to go before you let forth a string of invective that would shock those who previously underestimated your basic Aries traits.

Home and family are very dear to you, but you are more tolerant than some Aries types are inclined to be and you have a youthful zest for life that should stay with you no matter what age you manage to achieve. There is always something interesting to do and your mind is a constant stream of possibilities. This makes you very creative and you may also demonstrate a desire to look good at all times. You may not always be quite as confident as you appear to be, but few would guess the fact.

Aries with Scorpio Ascendant

The two very different faces of Mars come together in this potent, magnetic and quite awe-inspiring combination. Your natural inclination is towards secrecy and this fact, together with the natural attractions of the sensual Scorpio nature, makes you the object of great curiosity. This means that you will not go short of attention and should ensure that you are always being analysed by people who may never get to know you at all. At heart you prefer your own company, and yet life appears to find means to push you into the public gaze time and again. Most people with this combination ooze sex appeal and can use this fact as a stepping stone to personal success, yet without losing any integrity or loosening the cords of a deeply moralistic nature.

On those occasions when you do lose your temper, there isn't a character in the length and breadth of the zodiac who would have either the words or the courage to stand against the stream of invective that follows. On really rare occasions you might even scare yourself. As far as family members are concerned a simple look should be enough to show when you are not amused. Few people are left unmoved by your presence in their life.

Aries with Sagittarius Ascendant

What a lovely combination this can be, for the devil-may-care aspects of Sagittarius lighten the load of a sometimes too-serious Aries interior. Everything that glistens is not gold, though it's hard to convince you of the fact because, to mix metaphors, you can make a silk purse out of a sow's ear. Almost everyone loves you and in return you offer a friendship that is warm and protective, but not as demanding as sometimes tends to be the case with the Aries type. Relationships may be many and varied and there is often more than one major attachment in the life of those holding this combination. You will bring a breath of spring to any attachment, though you need to ensure that the person concerned is capable of keeping up with the hectic pace of your life.

It may appear from time to time that you are rather too trusting for your own good, though deep inside you are very astute and it seems that almost everything you undertake works out well in the end. This has nothing to do with native luck and is really down to the fact that you are much more calculating than might appear to be the case at first sight. As a parent you are protective yet offer sufficient room for self-expression.

Aries with Capricorn Ascendant

If ever anyone could be accused of setting off immediately, but slowly, it has to be you. These are very contradictory signs and the differences will express themselves in a variety of ways. One thing is certain, you have tremendous tenacity and will see a job through patiently from beginning to end, without tiring on the way, and ensuring that every detail is taken care of properly. This combination often bestows good health and a great capacity for continuity, particularly in terms of the length of life. You are certainly not as argumentative as the typical Aries, but you do know how to get your own way, which is just as well because you are usually thinking on behalf of everyone else and not just on your own account.

At home you can relax, which is a blessing for Aries, though in fact you seldom choose to do so because you always have some project or other on the go. You probably enjoy knocking down and rebuilding walls, though this is a practical tendency and not responsive to relationships, in which you are ardent and sincere. Impetuosity is as close to your heart as is the case for any type of Aries subject, though you certainly have the ability to appear patient and steady. But it's just a front, isn't it?

Aries with Aquarius Ascendant

The person standing on a soap box in the corner of the park, extolling the virtues of this or that, could quite easily be an Aries with an Aquarian Ascendant. You are certainly not averse to speaking your mind and you have plenty to talk about because you are the best social reformer and political animal of them all. Unorthodox in your approach, you have the ability to keep everyone guessing, except when it comes to getting your own way, for in this nobody doubts your natural abilities. You can put theories into practice very well and on the way you retain a sense of individuality that would shock more conservative types. It's true that a few people might find you a little difficult to approach and this is partly because you have an inner reserve and strength which is difficult forothers to fathom.

In the world at large you take your place at the front, as any good Arian should, and yet you offer room for others to share your platform. You keep up with the latest innovations and treat family members as the genuine friends that you believe them to be. Care needs to be taken when picking a life partner, for you are an original, and not just anyone could match the peculiarities thrown up by this astrological combination.

Aries with Pisces Ascendant

Although not an easy combination to deal with, the Aries with a Piscean Ascendant does, nevertheless, bring something very special to the world in the way of natural understanding allied to practical assistance. It's true that you can sometimes be a dreamer, but there is nothing wrong with that as long as you have the ability to turn some of your wishes into reality, and this you are easily able to do, usually for the sake of those around you. Conversation comes easily to you, though you also possess a slightly wistful and poetic side to your nature, which is attractive to the many people who call you a friend. A natural entertainer, you bring a sense of the comic to the often serious qualities of Aries, though without losing the determination that typifies the sign.

In relationships you are ardent, sincere and supportive, with a strong social conscience that sometimes finds you fighting the battles of the less privileged members of society. Family is important to you and this is a combination that invariably leads to parenthood. Away from the cut and thrust of everyday life you relax more fully and think about matters more deeply than more typical Aries types might.

THE MOON AND THE PART IT PLAYS IN YOUR LIFE

In astrology the Moon is probably the single most important heavenly body after the Sun. Its unique position, as partner to the Earth on its journey around the solar system, means that the Moon appears to pass through the signs of the zodiac extremely quickly. The zodiac position of the Moon at the time of your birth plays a great part in personal character and is especially significant in the build-up of your emotional nature.

Your Own Moon Sign

Discovering the position of the Moon at the time of your birth has always been notoriously difficult because tracking the complex zodiac positions of the Moon is not easy. This process has been reduced to three simple stages with our Lunar Tables. A breakdown of the Moon's zodiac positions can be found from page 35 onwards, so that once you know what your Moon Sign is, you can see what part this plays in the overall build-up of your personal character.

If you follow the instructions on the next page you will soon be able to work out exactly what zodiac sign the Moon occupied on the day that you were born and you can then go on to compare the reading for this position with those of your Sun sign and your Ascendant. It is partly the comparison between these three important positions that goes towards making you the unique individual you are.

HOW TO DISCOVER YOUR MOON SIGN

This is a three-stage process. You may need a pen and a piece of paper but if you follow the instructions below the process should only take a minute or so.

STAGE 1 First of all you need to know the Moon Age at the time of your birth. If you look at Moon Table 1, on page 33, you will find all the years between 1917 and 2015 down the left side. Find the year of your birth and then trace across to the right to the month of your birth. Where the two intersect you will find a number. This is the date of the New Moon in the month that you were born. You now need to count forward the number of days between the New Moon and your own birthday. For example, if the New Moon in the month of your birth was shown as being the 6th and you were born on the 20th, your Moon Age Day would be 14. If the New Moon in the month of your birth came after your birthday, you need to count forward from the New Moon in the previous month. If you were born in a Leap Year, remember to count the 29th February. You can tell if your birth year was a Leap Year if the last two digits can be divided by four. Whatever the result, jot this number down so that you do not forget it.

STAGE 2 Take a look at Moon Table 2 on page 34. Down the left hand column look for the date of your birth. Now trace across to the month of your birth. Where the two meet you will find a letter. Copy this letter down alongside your Moon Age Day.

STAGE 3 Moon Table 3 on page 34 will supply you with the zodiac sign the Moon occupied on the day of your birth. Look for your Moon Age Day down the left hand column and then for the letter you found in Stage 2. Where the two converge you will find a zodiac sign and this is the sign occupied by the Moon on the day that you were born.

Your Zodiac Moon Sign Explained

You will find a profile of all zodiac Moon Signs on pages 35 to 38, showing in yet another way how astrology helps to make you into the individual that you are. In each daily entry of the Astral Diary you can find the zodiac position of the Moon for every day of the year. This also allows you to discover your lunar birthdays. Since the Moon passes through all the signs of the zodiac in about a month, you can expect something like twelve lunar birthdays each year. At these times you are likely to be emotionally steady and able to make the sort of decisions that have real, lasting value.

MOON TABLE 1

YEAR	FEB	MAR	APR	YEAR	FEB	MAR	APR	YEAR	FEB	MAR	APR
1917	22	23	22	1950	16	18	17	1983	13	14	13
1918	11	12	11	1951	6	7	6	1984	1	2	1
1919	–	2/31	30	1952	25	25	24	1985	19	21	20
1920	19	20	18	1953	14	15	13	1986	9	10	9
1921	8	9	8	1954	3	5	3	1987	28	29	28
1922	26	28	27	1955	22	24	22	1988	17	18	16
1923	15	17	16	1956	11	12	11	1989	6	7	6
1924	5	5	4	1957	–	1/31	29	1990	25	26	25
1925	23	24	23	1958	18	20	19	1991	14	15	13
1926	12	14	12	1959	7	9	8	1992	3	4	3
1927	2	3	2	1960	26	27	26	1993	22	24	22
1928	19	21	20	1961	15	16	15	1994	10	12	11
1929	9	11	9	1962	5	6	5	1995	29	30	29
1930	28	30	28	1963	23	25	23	1996	18	19	18
1931	17	19	18	1964	13	14	12	1997	7	9	7
1932	6	7	6	1965	1	2	1	1998	26	27	26
1933	24	26	24	1966	19	21	20	1999	16	17	16
1934	14	15	13	1967	9	10	9	2000	5	6	4
1935	3	5	3	1968	28	29	28	2001	23	24	23
1936	22	23	21	1969	17	18	16	2002	12	13	12
1937	11	13	12	1970	6	7	6	2003	–	2	1
1938	–	2/31	30	1971	25	26	25	2004	20	21	19
1939	19	20	19	1972	14	15	13	2005	9	10	8
1940	8	9	7	1973	4	5	3	2006	28	29	27
1941	26	27	26	1974	22	24	22	2007	15	18	17
1942	15	16	15	1975	11	12	11	2008	6	7	6
1943	4	6	4	1976	29	30	29	2009	25	26	25
1944	24	24	22	1977	18	19	18	2010	14	15	14
1945	12	14	12	1978	7	9	7	2011	3	5	3
1946	2	3	2	1979	26	27	26	2012	22	22	21
1947	19	21	20	1980	15	16	15	2013	10	12	10
1948	9	11	9	1981	4	6	4	2014	1	1/31	30
1949	27	29	28	1982	23	24	23	2015	19	20	19

TABLE 2

DAY	MAR	APR
1	F	J
2	G	J
3	G	J
4	G	J
5	G	J
6	G	J
7	G	J
8	G	J
9	G	J
10	G	J
11	G	K
12	H	K
13	H	K
14	H	K
15	H	K
16	H	K
17	H	K
18	H	K
19	H	K
20	H	K
21	H	L
22	I	L
23	I	L
24	I	L
25	I	L
26	I	L
27	I	L
28	I	L
29	I	L
30	I	L
31	I	–

MOON TABLE 3

M/D	F	G	H	I	J	K	L
0	PI	PI	AR	AR	AR	TA	TA
1	PI	AR	AR	AR	TA	TA	TA
2	AR	AR	AR	TA	TA	TA	GE
3	AR	AR	TA	TA	TA	GE	GE
4	AR	TA	TA	GE	GE	GE	GE
5	TA	TA	GE	GE	GE	CA	CA
6	TA	GE	GE	GE	CA	CA	CA
7	GE	GE	GE	CA	CA	CA	LE
8	GE	GE	CA	CA	CA	LE	LE
9	CA	CA	CA	CA	LE	LE	VI
10	CA	CA	LE	LE	LE	VI	VI
11	CA	LE	LE	LE	VI	VI	VI
12	LE	LE	LE	VI	VI	VI	LI
13	LE	LE	VI	VI	VI	LI	LI
14	VI	VI	VI	LI	LI	LI	LI
15	VI	VI	LI	LI	LI	SC	SC
16	VI	LI	LI	LI	SC	SC	SC
17	LI	LI	LI	SC	SC	SC	SA
18	LI	LI	SC	SC	SC	SA	SA
19	LI	SC	SC	SC	SA	SA	SA
20	SC	SC	SA	SA	SA	CP	CP
21	SC	SA	SA	SA	CP	CP	CP
22	SC	SA	SA	CP	CP	CP	AQ
23	SA	SA	CP	CP	CP	AQ	AQ
24	SA	CP	CP	CP	AQ	AQ	AQ
25	CP	CP	AQ	AQ	AQ	PI	PI
26	CP	AQ	AQ	AQ	PI	PI	PI
27	AQ	AQ	AQ	PI	PI	PI	AR
28	AQ	AQ	PI	PI	PI	AR	AR
29	AQ	PI	PI	PI	AR	AR	AR

AR = Aries, TA = Taurus, GE = Gemini, CA = Cancer, LE = Leo, VI = Virgo, LI = Libra, SC = Scorpio, SA = Sagittarius, CP = Capricorn, AQ = Aquarius, PI = Pisces

MOON SIGNS

Moon in Aries

You have a strong imagination, courage, determination and a desire to do things in your own way and forge your own path through life.

Originality is a key attribute; you are seldom stuck for ideas although your mind is changeable and you could take the time to focus on individual tasks. Often quick-tempered, you take orders from few people and live life at a fast pace. Avoid health problems by taking regular time out for rest and relaxation.

Emotionally, it is important that you talk to those you are closest to and work out your true feelings. Once you discover that people are there to help, there is less necessity for you to do everything yourself.

Moon in Taurus

The Moon in Taurus gives you a courteous and friendly manner, which means you are likely to have many friends.

The good things in life mean a lot to you, as Taurus is an Earth sign that delights in experiences which please the senses. Hence you are probably a lover of good food and drink, which may in turn mean you need to keep an eye on the bathroom scales, especially as looking good is also important to you.

Emotionally you are fairly stable and you stick by your own standards. Taureans do not respond well to change. Intuition also plays an important part in your life.

Moon in Gemini

You have a warm-hearted character, sympathetic and eager to help others. At times reserved, you can also be articulate and chatty: this is part of the paradox of Gemini, which always brings duplicity to the nature. You are interested in current affairs, have a good intellect, and are good company and likely to have many friends. Most of your friends have a high opinion of you and would be ready to defend you should the need arise. However, this is usually unnecessary, as you are quite capable of defending yourself in any verbal confrontation.

Travel is important to your inquisitive mind and you find intellectual stimulus in mixing with people from different cultures. You also gain much from reading, writing and the arts but you do need plenty of rest and relaxation in order to avoid fatigue.

Moon in Cancer

The Moon in Cancer at the time of birth is a fortunate position as Cancer is the Moon's natural home. This means that the qualities of compassion and understanding given by the Moon are especially enhanced in your nature, and you are friendly and sociable and cope well with emotional pressures. You cherish home and family life, and happily do the domestic tasks. Your surroundings are important to you and you hate squalor and filth. You are likely to have a love of music and poetry.

Your basic character, although at times changeable like the Moon itself, depends on symmetry. You aim to make your surroundings comfortable and harmonious, for yourself and those close to you.

Moon in Leo

The best qualities of the Moon and Leo come together to make you warm-hearted, fair, ambitious and self-confident. With good organisational abilities, you invariably rise to a position of responsibility in your chosen career. This is fortunate as you don't enjoy being an 'also-ran' and would rather be an important part of a small organisation than a menial in a large one.

You should be lucky in love, and happy, provided you put in the effort to make a comfortable home for yourself and those close to you. It is likely that you will have a love of pleasure, sport, music and literature. Life brings you many rewards, most of them as a direct result of your own efforts, although you may be luckier than average and ready to make the best of any situation.

Moon in Virgo

You are endowed with good mental abilities and a keen receptive memory, but you are never ostentatious or pretentious. Naturally quite reserved, you still have many friends, especially of the opposite sex. Marital relationships must be discussed carefully and worked at so that they remain harmonious, as personal attachments can be a problem if you do not give them your full attention.

Talented and persevering, you possess artistic qualities and are a good homemaker. Earning your honours through genuine merit, you work long and hard towards your objectives but show little pride in your achievements. Many short journeys will be undertaken in your life.

Moon in Libra

With the Moon in Libra you are naturally popular and make friends easily. People like you, probably more than you realise, you bring fun to a party and are a natural diplomat. For all its good points, Libra is not the most stable of astrological signs and, as a result, your emotions can be a little unstable too. Therefore, although the Moon in Libra is said to be good for love and marriage, your Sun sign and Rising sign will have an important effect on your emotional and loving qualities.

You must remember to relate to others in your decision-making. Co-operation is crucial because Libra represents the 'balance' of life that can only be achieved through harmonious relationships. Conformity is not easy for you because Libra, an Air sign, likes its independence.

Moon in Scorpio

Some people might call you pushy. In fact, all you really want to do is to live life to the full and protect yourself and your family from the pressures of life. Take care to avoid giving the impression of being sarcastic or impulsive and use your energies wisely and constructively.

You have great courage and you invariably achieve your goals by force of personality and sheer effort. You are fond of mystery and are good at predicting the outcome of situations and events. Travel experiences can be beneficial to you.

You may experience problems if you do not take time to examine your motives in a relationship, and also if you allow jealousy, always a feature of Scorpio, to cloud your judgement.

Moon in Sagittarius

The Moon in Sagittarius helps to make you a generous individual with humanitarian qualities and a kind heart. Restlessness may be intrinsic as your mind is seldom still. Perhaps because of this, you have a need for change that could lead you to several major moves during your adult life. You are not afraid to stand your ground when you know your judgement is right, you speak directly and have good intuition.

At work you are quick, efficient and versatile and so you make an ideal employee. You need work to be intellectually demanding and do not enjoy tedious routines.

In relationships, you anger quickly if faced with stupidity or deception, though you are just as quick to forgive and forget. Emotionally, there are times when your heart rules your head.

Moon in Capricorn

The Moon in Capricorn makes you popular and likely to come into the public eye in some way. The watery Moon is not entirely comfortable in the Earth sign of Capricorn and this may lead to some difficulties in the early years of life. An initial lack of creative ability and indecision must be overcome before the true qualities of patience and perseverance inherent in Capricorn can show through.

You have good administrative ability and are a capable worker, and if you are careful you can accumulate wealth. But you must be cautious and take professional advice in partnerships, as you are open to deception. You may be interested in social or welfare work, which suit your organisational skills and sympathy for others.

Moon in Aquarius

The Moon in Aquarius makes you an active and agreeable person with a friendly, easy-going nature. Sympathetic to the needs of others, you flourish in a laid-back atmosphere. You are broad-minded, fair and open to suggestion, although sometimes you have an unconventional quality which others can find hard to understand.

You are interested in the strange and curious, and in old articles and places. You enjoy trips to these places and gain much from them. Political, scientific and educational work interests you and you might choose a career in science or technology.

Money-wise, you make gains through innovation and concentration and Lunar Aquarians often tackle more than one job at a time. In love you are kind and honest.

Moon in Pisces

You have a kind, sympathetic nature, somewhat retiring at times, but you always take account of others' feelings and help when you can.

Personal relationships may be problematic, but as life goes on you can learn from your experiences and develop a better understanding of yourself and the world around you.

You have a fondness for travel, appreciate beauty and harmony and hate disorder and strife. You may be fond of literature and would make a good writer or speaker yourself. You have a creative imagination and may come across as an incurable romantic. You have strong intuition, maybe bordering on a mediumistic quality, which sets you apart from the mass. You may not be rich in cash terms, but your personal gifts are worth more than gold.

ARIES IN LOVE

Discover how compatible in love you are with people from the same and other signs of the zodiac. Five stars equals a match made in heaven!

Aries meets Aries

This could be an all-or-nothing pairing. Both parties are from a dominant sign, so someone will have to be flexible in order to maintain personal harmony. Both know what they want out of life, and may have trouble overcoming any obstacles a relationship creates. This is a good physical pairing, with a chemistry that few other matches enjoy to the same level. Attitude is everything, but at least there is a mutual admiration that makes gazing at your partner like looking in the mirror. Star rating: ****

Aries meets Taurus

This is a match that has been known to work very well. Aries brings dynamism and ambition, while Taurus has the patience to see things through logically. Such complementary views work equally well in a relationship or in the office. There is mutual respect, but sometimes a lack of total understanding. The romantic needs of each are quite different, but both are still fulfilled. They can live easily in domestic harmony which is very important but, interestingly, Aries may be the loser in battles of will. Star rating: ***

Aries meets Gemini

Don't expect peace and harmony with this combination, although what comes along instead might make up for any disagreements. Gemini has a very fertile imagination, while Aries has the tenacity to make reality from fantasy. Combined, they have a sizzling relationship. There are times when both parties could explode with indignation and something has to give. But even if there are clashes, making them up will always be most enjoyable! Mutual financial success is likely in this match. Star rating: ****

Aries meets Cancer

A potentially one-sided pairing, it often appears that the Cancerian is brow-beaten by the far more dominant Arian. So much depends on the patience of the Cancerian individual, because if good psychology is present – who knows? But beware, Aries, you may find your partner too passive, and constantly having to take the lead can be wearing – even for you. A prolonged trial period would be advantageous, as the match could easily go either way. When it does work, though, this relationship is usually contented. Star rating: ***

Aries meets Leo

Stand by for action and make sure the house is sound-proof. Leo is a lofty idealist and there is always likely to be friction when two Fire signs meet. To compensate, there is much mutual admiration, together with a desire to please. Where there are shared incentives, the prognosis is good but it's important not to let little irritations blow up. Both signs want to have their own way and this is a sure cause of trouble. There might not be much patience here, but there is plenty of action. Star rating: *****

Aries meets Virgo

Neither of these signs really understands the other, and that could easily lead to a clash. Virgo is so pedantic, which will drive Aries up the wall, while Aries always wants to be moving on to the next objective, before Virgo is even settled with the last one. It will take time for these two to get to know each other, but this is a great business matching. If a personal relationship is seen in these terms then the prognosis can be good, but on the whole, this is not an inspiring match. Star rating: ***

Aries meets Libra

These signs are zodiac opposites which means a make-or-break situation. The match will either be a great success or a dismal failure. Why? Well Aries finds it difficult to understand the flighty Air-sign tendencies of Libra, whilst the natural balance of Libra contradicts the unorthodox Arian methods. Any flexibility will come from Libra, which may mean that things work out for a while, but Libra only has so much patience and it may eventually run out. In the end, Aries may be just too bossy for an independent but sensitive sign like Libra. Star rating: **

Aries meets Scorpio

There can be great affection here, even if the two zodiac signs are so very different. The common link is the planet Mars, which plays a part in both these natures. Although Aries is, outwardly, the most dominant, Scorpio people are among the most powerful to be found anywhere. This quiet determination is respected by Aries. Aries will satisfy the passionate side of Scorpio, particularly with instruction from Scorpio. There are mysteries here which will add spice to life. The few arguments that do occur are likely to be awe-inspiring. Star rating: ****

Aries meets Sagittarius

This can be one of the most favourable matches of them all. Both Aries and Sagittarius are Fire signs, which often leads to clashes of will, but this pair find a mutual understanding. Sagittarius helps Aries to develop a better sense of humour, while Aries teaches the Archer about consistency on the road to success. Some patience is called for on both sides, but these people have a natural liking for each other. Add this to growing love and you have a long-lasting combination that is hard to beat. Star rating: *****

Aries meets Capricorn

Capricorn works conscientiously to achieve its objectives and so can be the perfect companion for Aries. The Ram knows how to achieve but not how to consolidate, so the two signs have a great deal to offer one another practically. There may not be fireworks and it's sometimes doubtful how well they know each other, but it may not matter. Aries is outwardly hot but inwardly cool, whilst Capricorn can appear low key but be a furnace underneath. Such a pairing can gradually find contentment, though both parties may wonder how this is so. Star rating: ****

Aries meets Aquarius

Aquarius is an Air sign, and Air and Fire often work well together, but perhaps not in the case of Aries and Aquarius. The average Aquarian lives in what the Ram sees as a fantasy world, so without a sufficiently good meeting of minds, compromise may be lacking. Of course, almost anything is possible, and the dominant side of Aries could be trained by the devil-may-care attitude of Aquarius. There are meeting points but they are difficult to establish. However, given sufficient time and an open mind on both sides, a degree of happiness is possible. Star rating: **

Aries meets Pisces

Still waters run deep, and they don't come much deeper than Pisces. Although these signs share the same quadrant of the zodiac, they have little in common. Pisces is a dreamer, a romantic idealist with steady and spiritual goals. Aries needs to be on the move, and has very different ideals. It's hard to see how a relationship could develop because the outlook on life is so different but, with patience, especially from Aries, there is a chance that things might work out. Pisces needs incentive, and Aries may be the sign to offer it. Star rating: **

VENUS: THE PLANET OF LOVE

If you look up at the sky around sunset or sunrise you will often see Venus in close attendance to the Sun. It is arguably one of the most beautiful sights of all and there is little wonder that historically it became associated with the goddess of love. But although Venus does play an important part in the way you view love and in the way others see you romantically, this is only one of the spheres of influence that it enjoys in your overall character.

Venus has a part to play in the more cultured side of your life and has much to do with your appreciation of art, literature, music and general creativity. Even the way you look is responsive to the part of the zodiac that Venus occupied at the start of your life, though this fact is also down to your Sun sign and Ascending sign. If, at the time you were born, Venus occupied one of the more gregarious zodiac signs, you will be more likely to wear your heart on your sleeve, as well as to be more attracted to entertainment, social gatherings and good company. If on the other hand Venus occupied a quiet zodiac sign at the time of your birth, you would tend to be more retiring and less willing to shine in public situations.

It's good to know what part the planet Venus plays in your life for it can have a great bearing on the way you appear to the rest of the world and since we all have to mix with others, you can learn to make the very best of what Venus has to offer you.

One of the great complications in the past has always been trying to establish exactly what zodiac position Venus enjoyed when you were born because the planet is notoriously difficult to track. However, we have solved that problem by creating a table that is exclusive to your Sun sign, which you will find on the following page.

Establishing your Venus sign could not be easier. Just look up the year of your birth on the following page and you will see a sign of the zodiac. This was the sign that Venus occupied in the period covered by your sign in that year. If Venus occupied more than one sign during the period, this is indicated by the date on which the sign changed, and the name of the new sign. For instance, if you were born in 1950, Venus was in Aquarius until the 7th April, after which time it was in Pisces. If you were born before 7th April your Venus sign is Aquarius, if you were born on or after 7th April, your Venus sign is Pisces. Once you have established the position of Venus at the time of your birth, you can then look in the pages which follow to see how this has a bearing on your life as a whole.

1917 PISCES / 28.3 ARIES
1918 AQUARIUS / 5.4 PISCES
1919 ARIES / 24.3 TAURUS
1920 PISCES / 14.4 ARIES
1921 TAURUS
1922 ARIES / 13.4 TAURUS
1923 AQUARIUS / 1.4 PISCES
1924 TAURUS / 6.4 GEMINI
1925 PISCES / 28.3 ARIES
1926 AQUARIUS / 6.4 PISCES
1927 ARIES / 24.3 TAURUS
1928 PISCES / 13.4 ARIES
1929 TAURUS / 20.4 ARIES
1930 ARIES / 13.4 TAURUS
1931 AQUARIUS / 31.3 PISCES
1932 TAURUS / 6.4 GEMINI
1933 PISCES / 27.3 ARIES
1934 AQUARIUS / 6.4 PISCES
1935 ARIES / 23.3 TAURUS
1936 PISCES / 13.4 ARIES
1937 TAURUS / 14.4 ARIES
1938 ARIES / 12.4 TAURUS
1939 AQUARIUS / 31.3 PISCES
1940 TAURUS / 5.4 GEMINI
1941 PISCES / 26.3 ARIES / 20.4 TAURUS
1942 AQUARIUS / 7.4 PISCES
1943 ARIES / 23.3 TAURUS
1944 PISCES / 12.4 ARIES
1945 TAURUS / 8.4 ARIES
1946 ARIES / 12.4 TAURUS
1947 AQUARIUS / 30.3 PISCES
1948 TAURUS / 5.4 GEMINI
1949 PISCES / 25.3 ARIES / 20.4 TAURUS
1950 AQUARIUS / 7.4 PISCES
1951 ARIES / 22.3 TAURUS
1952 PISCES / 12.4 ARIES
1953 TAURUS / 1.4 ARIES
1954 ARIES / 11.4 TAURUS
1955 AQUARIUS / 30.3 PISCES
1956 TAURUS / 4.4 GEMINI
1957 PISCES / 25.3 ARIES / 19.4 TAURUS
1958 AQUARIUS / 8.4 PISCES
1959 ARIES / 22.3 TAURUS
1960 PISCES / 11.4 ARIES
1961 ARIES
1962 ARIES / 11.4 TAURUS
1963 AQUARIUS / 29.3 PISCES
1964 TAURUS / 4.4 GEMINI
1965 PISCES / 24.3 ARIES / 19.4 TAURUS
1966 AQUARIUS / 8.4 PISCES
1967 TAURUS / 20.4 GEMINI
1968 PISCES / 10.4 ARIES
1969 ARIES
1970 ARIES / 10.4 TAURUS
1971 AQUARIUS / 29.3 PISCES
1972 TAURUS / 3.4 GEMINI
1973 PISCES / 24.3 ARIES / 18.4 TAURUS
1974 AQUARIUS / 8.4 PISCES
1975 TAURUS / 19.4 GEMINI
1976 PISCES / 10.4 ARIES
1977 ARIES
1978 ARIES / 10.4 TAURUS
1979 AQUARIUS / 28.3 PISCES
1980 TAURUS / 3.4 GEMINI
1981 PISCES / 23.3 ARIES / 18.4 TAURUS
1982 AQUARIUS / 9.4 PISCES
1983 TAURUS / 19.4 GEMINI
1984 PISCES / 9.4 ARIES
1985 ARIES
1986 ARIES / 9.4 TAURUS
1987 AQUARIUS / 28.3 PISCES
1988 TAURUS / 2.4 GEMINI
1989 PISCES / 23.3 ARIES / 17.4 TAURUS
1990 AQUARIUS / 9.4 PISCES
1991 TAURUS / 18.4 GEMINI
1992 PISCES / 9.4 ARIES
1993 ARIES
1994 ARIES / 9.4 TAURUS
1995 AQUARIUS / 27.3 PISCES
1996 TAURUS / 2.4 GEMINI
1997 PISCES / 22.3 ARIES / 17.4 TAURUS
1998 AQUARIUS / 9.4 PISCES
1999 TAURUS / 18.4 GEMINI
2000 PISCES / 9.4 ARIES
2001 ARIES
2002 ARIES / 7.4 TAURUS
2003 AQUARIUS / 27.3 PISCES
2004 TAURUS / 1.4 GEMINI
2005 PISCES/22.3 ARIES
2006 AQUARIUS/7.4 PISCES
2007 TAURUS / 16.4 GEMINI
2008 PISCES / 9.4 ARIES
2009 ARIES
2010 ARIES / 7.4 TAURUS
2011 AQUARIUS / 27.3 PISCES
2012 TAURUS / 1.4 GEMINI
2013 PISCES / 22.3 ARIES
2014 AQUARIUS / 7.4 PISCES
2015 TAURUS / 16.4 GEMINI

VENUS THROUGH THE ZODIAC SIGNS

Venus in Aries

Amongst other things, the position of Venus in Aries indicates a fondness for travel, music and all creative pursuits. Your nature tends to be affectionate and you would try not to create confusion or difficulty for others if it could be avoided. Many people with this planetary position have a great love of the theatre, and mental stimulation is of the greatest importance. Early romantic attachments are common with Venus in Aries, so it is very important to establish a genuine sense of romantic continuity. Early marriage is not recommended, especially if it is based on sympathy. You may give your heart a little too readily on occasions.

Venus in Taurus

You are capable of very deep feelings and your emotions tend to last for a very long time. This makes you a trusting partner and lover, whose constancy is second to none. In life you are precise and careful and always try to do things the right way. Although this means an ordered life, which you are comfortable with, it can also lead you to be rather too fussy for your own good. Despite your pleasant nature, you are very fixed in your opinions and quite able to speak your mind. Others are attracted to you and historical astrologers always quoted this position of Venus as being very fortunate in terms of marriage. However, if you find yourself involved in a failed relationship, it could take you a long time to trust again.

Venus in Gemini

As with all associations related to Gemini, you tend to be quite versatile, anxious for change and intelligent in your dealings with the world at large. You may gain money from more than one source but you are equally good at spending it. There is an inference here that you are a good communicator, via either the written or the spoken word, and you love to be in the company of interesting people. Always on the look-out for culture, you may also be very fond of music, and love to indulge the curious and cultured side of your nature. In romance you tend to have more than one relationship and could find yourself associated with someone who has previously been a friend or even a distant relative.

Venus in Cancer

You often stay close to home because you are very fond of family and enjoy many of your most treasured moments when you are with those you love. Being naturally sympathetic, you will always do anything you can to support those around you, even people you hardly know at all. This charitable side of your nature is your most noticeable trait and is one of the reasons why others are naturally so fond of you. Being receptive and in some cases even psychic, you can see through to the soul of most of those with whom you come into contact. You may not commence too many romantic attachments but when you do give your heart, it tends to be unconditionally.

Venus in Leo

It must become quickly obvious to almost anyone you meet that you are kind, sympathetic and yet determined enough to stand up for anyone or anything that is truly important to you. Bright and sunny, you warm the world with your natural enthusiasm and would rarely do anything to hurt those around you, or at least not intentionally. In romance you are ardent and sincere, though some may find your style just a little overpowering. Gains come through your contacts with other people and this could be especially true with regard to romance, for love and money often come hand in hand for those who were born with Venus in Leo. People claim to understand you, though you are more complex than you seem.

Venus in Virgo

Your nature could well be fairly quiet no matter what your Sun sign might be, though this fact often manifests itself as an inner peace and would not prevent you from being basically sociable. Some delays and even the odd disappointment in love cannot be ruled out with this planetary position, though it's a fact that you will usually find the happiness you look for in the end. Catapulting yourself into romantic entanglements that you know to be rather ill-advised is not sensible, and it would be better to wait before you committed yourself exclusively to any one person. It is the essence of your nature to serve the world at large and through doing so it is possible that you will attract money at some stage in your life.

Venus in Libra

Venus is very comfortable in Libra and bestows upon those people who have this planetary position a particular sort of kindness that is easy to recognise. This is a very good position for all sorts of friendships and also for romantic attachments that usually bring much joy into your life. Few individuals with Venus in Libra would avoid marriage and since you are capable of great depths of love, it is likely that you will find a contented personal life. You like to mix with people of integrity and intelligence but don't take kindly to scruffy surroundings or work that means getting your hands too dirty. Careful speculation, good business dealings and money through marriage all seem fairly likely.

Venus in Scorpio

You are quite open and tend to spend money quite freely, even on those occasions when you don't have very much. Although your intentions are always good, there are times when you get yourself in to the odd scrape and this can be particularly true when it comes to romance, which you may come to late or from a rather unexpected direction. Certainly you have the power to be happy and to make others contented on the way, but you find the odd stumbling block on your journey through life and it could seem that you have to work harder than those around you. As a result of this, you gain a much deeper understanding of the true value of personal happiness than many people ever do, and are likely to achieve true contentment in the end.

Venus in Sagittarius

You are lighthearted, cheerful and always able to see the funny side of any situation. These facts enhance your popularity, which is especially high with members of the opposite sex. You should never have to look too far to find romantic interest in your life, though it is just possible that you might be too willing to commit yourself before you are certain that the person in question is right for you. Part of the problem here extends to other areas of life too. The fact is that you like variety in everything and so can tire of situations that fail to offer it. All the same, if you choose wisely and learn to understand your restless side, then great happiness can be yours.

Venus in Capricorn

The most notable trait that comes from Venus in this position is that it makes you trustworthy and able to take on all sorts of responsibilities in life. People are instinctively fond of you and love you all the more because you are always ready to help those who are in any form of need. Social and business popularity can be yours and there is a magnetic quality to your nature that is particularly attractive in a romantic sense. Anyone who wants a partner for a lover, a spouse and a good friend too would almost certainly look in your direction. Constancy is the hallmark of your nature and unfaithfulness would go right against the grain. You might sometimes be a little too trusting.

Venus in Aquarius

This location of Venus offers a fondness for travel and a desire to try out something new at every possible opportunity. You are extremely easy to get along with and tend to have many friends from varied backgrounds, classes and inclinations. You like to live a distinct sort of life and gain a great deal from moving about, both in a career sense and with regard to your home. It is not out of the question that you could form a romantic attachment to someone who comes from far away or be attracted to a person of a distinctly artistic and original nature. What you cannot stand is jealousy, for you have friends of both sexes and would want to keep things that way.

Venus in Pisces

The first thing people tend to notice about you is your wonderful, warm smile. Being very charitable by nature you will do anything to help others, even if you don't know them well. Much of your life may be spent sorting out situations for other people, but it is very important to feel that you are living for yourself too. In the main, you remain cheerful, and tend to be quite attractive to members of the opposite sex. Where romantic attachments are concerned, you could be drawn to people who are significantly older or younger than yourself or to someone with a unique career or point of view. It might be best for you to avoid marrying whilst you are still very young.

ARIES:
2014 DIARY PAGES

October 2014

1 WEDNESDAY *Moon Age Day 7 Moon Sign Sagittarius*

Where practical matters are concerned, the focus is on your determination to do things in more or less your own way. There's an emphasis on your creativity and your desire to get ahead, though you can't expect everything to go your way. What you do possess is the ability to push over obstacles if they happen to appear.

2 THURSDAY *Moon Age Day 8 Moon Sign Capricorn*

Trends now benefit partnerships, whether they are of a practical, professional or personal nature. Seeing the other person's point of view isn't always your strong point, but you are encouraged to do so at present. Routine holds no appeal for you this Thursday, and doing whatever takes your fancy is far more suited to your frame of mind.

3 FRIDAY *Moon Age Day 9 Moon Sign Capricorn*

Today is about keeping the wheels of progress turning, and showing that you are willing to change with the wind. This isn't always the case with Aries, which can be the most stubborn of all the zodiac signs – with the possible exception of Taurus! All manner of people fascinate you today, and for a host of different reasons.

4 SATURDAY *Moon Age Day 10 Moon Sign Aquarius*

The more you can be in the company of interesting people today, the greater is the your potential for joy and happiness. Rather than confining your interests in any way, it pays to spread yourself across a range of different subjects. Romance is once again emphasised, spurred on by your present light-hearted attitude.

5 SUNDAY ☿ *Moon Age Day 11 Moon Sign Aquarius*

This is an excellent time to focus on the unusual – or even the downright peculiar. There's no reason to doubt your intuition at this stage because it is well accented, and unlikely to lead you in the wrong direction. Seeking support from friends is all very well, though not if they are preoccupied with other matters.

6 MONDAY ☿ *Moon Age Day 12 Moon Sign Pisces*

Beware of letting good ideas languish today simply because you don't seem to have what it takes to make them work. Instead of taking no for an answer, you can afford to push your weight around a little. This is not something that comes hard to Aries, and it could help you to gain a positive listening ear from someone important.

7 TUESDAY ☿ *Moon Age Day 13 Moon Sign Pisces*

Despite a slightly quieter frame of mind, social impulses are strong and you should be making the most of opportunities to mix in a wealth of different directions. By all means stand up for your rights if you think they are being ignored, but don't push issues too strongly. There is a chance that you could be wrong!

8 WEDNESDAY ☿ *Moon Age Day 14 Moon Sign Aries*

The Moon returns to your zodiac sign, reinforcing your will and making it possible to move some sizeable mountains. Whether your personal circumstances favour this interlude on this mid-week day remains to be seen, but you certainly should not doubt either your own tenacity or your practical abilities now.

9 THURSDAY ☿ *Moon Age Day 15 Moon Sign Aries*

The further you can reach, the more you can accomplish today. That doesn't mean you should knock yourself out, which isn't exactly the right recipe for success in the longer term. You need pace and a good deal of common sense if you want to make the most of every opportunity, of which there could be many now.

10 FRIDAY ☿ *Moon Age Day 16 Moon Sign Taurus*

You need to keep a variety of interests on the go now if at all possible. Don't be too quick to make dramatic changes, especially to your professional life. Today responds best to a gentle touch on the tiller and the certain knowledge that every action you take might have a slightly adverse bearing on others.

11 SATURDAY ☿ *Moon Age Day 17 Moon Sign Taurus*

This would be an ideal day for tackling financial complexities, even if this doesn't appear to be the case during the first part of Saturday. A shopping spree might suit your present frame of mind and would offer you the chance to seek out plenty of potential bargains well ahead of Christmas.

12 SUNDAY ☿ *Moon Age Day 18 Moon Sign Gemini*

Even if you don't want to believe everything you hear today, you need to bear in mind that at least some of it will be true. Trends encourage you to allow your confidence to grow in a professional sense, but don't be too clever for your own good. It's important to check and recheck all facts and figures before proceeding.

13 MONDAY ☿ *Moon Age Day 19 Moon Sign Gemini*

The spotlight is now on emotional issues that need to be dealt with, though if you are busy in a practical sense this may not be your top priority. You need to recognise that others have specific matters they wish to address. A good old-fashioned heart-to-heart talk could work wonders under current influences.

14 TUESDAY ☿ *Moon Age Day 20 Moon Sign Cancer*

It appears that a diversity of interests works best at this stage of the month, and this would certainly seem to be what the present planetary line-up is indicating. However, there may be specific issues that are presently difficult to avoid. Turning your attention towards them won't be too appealing, but it could be necessary.

15 WEDNESDAY ☿ *Moon Age Day 21 Moon Sign Cancer*

It's time to come up with some good ideas on the financial front, and to implement them just as quickly as you can. This is an ideal interlude for taking any problem by the scruff of the neck and shaking it into order. You needn't take no for an answer from others, particularly if you are able to override their opinions gently.

16 THURSDAY ☿ *Moon Age Day 22 Moon Sign Cancer*

Trends assist you to create a favourable impression on others, which should aid your progress no end. If you can impress those who have influence, then so much the better. In a home-related sense you need to avoid accidentally upsetting anyone who is genuinely doing their best. Sensitivity is the order of the day.

17 FRIDAY ☿ *Moon Age Day 23 Moon Sign Leo*

Don't be afraid to rely on the good offices of others, even those you don't like very much. This can offer you a chance to reassess your opinion of them. Be ready to respond to the variable attitudes of family members, and recognise that it's not possible for you to know how anyone is likely to jump under different circumstances.

18 SATURDAY ☿ *Moon Age Day 24 Moon Sign Leo*

This would be an ideal time for domestic planning of almost any sort. It's fine to focus on housework and new ideas for your home, though they might have to be fitted in with your general routine because professional aspects are present too. All in all a positive day, but one that works best if you are prepared to organise things.

19 SUNDAY ☿ *Moon Age Day 25 Moon Sign Virgo*

The accent for Sunday is clearly on romance and fun. You can perfect your creative skills by organising gatherings or social functions, while at the same time feathering your nest in more practical ways. Mixing business with pleasure is the great forte of your zodiac sign, and you need to demonstrate this fact today.

20 MONDAY ☿ *Moon Age Day 26 Moon Sign Virgo*

Socially and romantically you should be on top form. You have scope to ensure that just about everything you do at the moment is interesting and rewarding. Does it feel as though not everyone is on your side? If so, simply stand back and look at situations from a distance. In reality, the world is your oyster right now.

21 TUESDAY ☿ *Moon Age Day 27 Moon Sign Virgo*

The signs are that engaging in intellectual pursuits would be a valuable use of your time and talents. Your mind should be razor sharp, encouraging you to pit yourself against almost anyone. Routines might seem rather tedious, though they do have their value at the moment, and should not simply be ignored.

22 WEDNESDAY ☿ *Moon Age Day 28 Moon Sign Libra*

The arrival of the lunar low brings a phase in which a less active approach is encouraged for a couple of days. Be careful who you trust today. Even though it is the essence of your nature to give others the benefit of the doubt, there may be certain individuals around at present who are not quite what they seem.

23 THURSDAY ☿ *Moon Age Day 0 Moon Sign Libra*

If general energies are flagging at this time, there's nothing wrong with deliberately choosing to take a rest. Conforming to the expectations of others will be hardest of all, so retreating into your shell somewhat could certainly be a valid response. Extra care is recommended when dealing with mechanical objects at this time.

24 FRIDAY ☿ *Moon Age Day 1 Moon Sign Scorpio*

It's possible that there may be situations around today that could frustrate you, which is why it you need to be prepared to take a very steady path through life right now. Avoid getting on the wrong side of people around you. It's worth remembering that any one of them might prove to be extremely useful to you in the near future.

25 SATURDAY ☿ *Moon Age Day 2 Moon Sign Scorpio*

This is a weekend during which your interests are best served by finding time for family members and for dealing with issues around your home. Even Aries is not encouraged to wander too far, unless any specific journey has been planned for some time. Also, don't be surprised if the attitude of a friend seems rather mysterious.

26 SUNDAY *Moon Age Day 3 Moon Sign Scorpio*

Mental stimulus may be gained from a number of different directions and helps you to push forward at this time. There is room to grow and to think up interesting new ideas that are going to be extremely useful as this year comes to an end. Don't be too quick to judge the actions of a relative or a very close friend.

27 MONDAY *Moon Age Day 4 Moon Sign Sagittarius*

Working especially hard today should pay significant dividends in the medium term, particularly if you are able to achieve a better relationship with co-workers at the start of the week. It's important to recognise that even if comfort isn't at the forefront of your mind right now, it may be important to those around you.

28 TUESDAY *Moon Age Day 5 Moon Sign Sagittarius*

Romantically and personally, you have what it takes to make this one of the most enjoyable times during the whole of October. New relationships could be on the cards for those who have been looking for love, and you shouldn't have any difficulty at all charming the birds down from the trees, either now or tomorrow.

29 WEDNESDAY *Moon Age Day 6 Moon Sign Capricorn*

Once again the romantic qualities within your nature are stimulated, as is your natural charm. You can use these influences to ensure that you are flavour of the month with a number of different people. This might even include those you haven't seen eye to eye with in the past.

30 THURSDAY *Moon Age Day 7 Moon Sign Capricorn*

There is a strong sense of togetherness around, which is especially emphasised in your love life today. Relating to people from your past should now also be easier, and you might even be in a position to bury a hatchet that has been a problem for quite some time. Arbitrating between others is also possible around now.

31 FRIDAY *Moon Age Day 8 Moon Sign Aquarius*

Your need for family and emotional security is emphasised, bringing you to the end of October in a slightly 'mixed' mood. The material and practical aspects of life are still important, but a degree of deep thinking is also indicated, and you should be aware that this has potential to get in the way of intended successes.

♈

November

2014

1 SATURDAY *Moon Age Day 9 Moon Sign Aquarius*

The weekend offers a chance to stand aside from the purely practical aspects of life, assisting you to concentrate on more emotional or even spiritual matters. Although you can benefit from a great sense of freedom around now, this doesn't mean you are obliged to travel further than is strictly necessary.

2 SUNDAY *Moon Age Day 10 Moon Sign Pisces*

Although you are now encouraged to surround yourself with things that are familiar, you can also afford to stretch the bounds of probability. Acting on impulse is all very well, though it could lead to a few mistakes being made. Forcing yourself to be logical and methodical isn't easy, but might be necessary.

3 MONDAY *Moon Age Day 11 Moon Sign Pisces*

The current emphasis is firmly on the things you choose to do with family members, especially your partner, and this could make the beginning of this week rather unusual for you. You can afford to put the strictly material considerations of life on hold as your twelfth-house Moon allows a softening of your Fire-sign nature.

4 TUESDAY *Moon Age Day 12 Moon Sign Aries*

Confidence is well marked as the lunar high arrives, and your need for forward progress allows you to catapult out of the depths your mind has reached in recent days. Now it's action all the way and you should be showing an extremely adventurous and determined face to the world at large. This is the normal Aries!

5 WEDNESDAY *Moon Age Day 13 Moon Sign Aries*

A period of transformation is available, and this is a long-term affair with quite far-reaching implications. It won't be until December that you fully appreciate some of the potentials now developing in your life. You would be wise to avoid arguments at a personal level and simply get on with what is required.

6 THURSDAY *Moon Age Day 14 Moon Sign Taurus*

If you're now on a personal voyage of discovery, part of the process could involve discovering facts and figures that give you a greater understanding of the way the world works. With a renewed sense of wonder and plenty of incentive, it looks as though you can achieve a rather special day – if a somewhat odd one!

7 FRIDAY *Moon Age Day 15 Moon Sign Taurus*

Make the most of what has potential to be one of the best days of November when it comes to career interests. However, you do need to be careful to diversify when necessary, and should not allow yourself to get stuck in any sort of rut. Why not seek some sound professional advice from someone in the know?

8 SATURDAY *Moon Age Day 16 Moon Sign Taurus*

Be prepared to tap into the help that is on offer when it comes to professional developments. All the same, it's also important to focus on home-based issues, which might include convincing family members that your point of view is the most valid. Don't be too quick to take offence in simple discussions.

9 SUNDAY *Moon Age Day 17 Moon Sign Gemini*

News you gather from far off can be used as a good stimulus in your personal life. Getting in touch with someone you haven't heard from for ages would be no bad thing, and could offer scope for a get-together. At home you need to show a very positive attitude towards new incentives, even if you have doubts about them.

10 MONDAY *Moon Age Day 18 Moon Sign Gemini*

This is an ideal time to decide whether you should jettison some aspects of life that are now of little or no use to you. Concentrate on the matter at hand, even if this seems quite difficult at present. When the practicalities are out of the way, it's up to you to make the most of very favourable social and romantic trends.

11 TUESDAY *Moon Age Day 19 Moon Sign Cancer*

You may be too busy to focus much on money in a day-to-day sense, and yet it is very important to do so. Those Aries subjects who take a responsible attitude to life will probably already be planning for Christmas, and today would be ideal for shopping or for looking carefully at exactly what is available to spend.

12 WEDNESDAY *Moon Age Day 20 Moon Sign Cancer*

Today can offer you scope to achieve satisfactory accomplishments, even if situations are not as clear-cut as you might wish. Getting to the nitty-gritty of specific matters may not be at all easy, but you do have it in your power to show a determined and positive face regarding matters that are going to be important later.

13 THURSDAY *Moon Age Day 21 Moon Sign Leo*

This would be another favourable time to broaden your horizons, though you may decide not to start doing so until the middle of the day. Creature comforts are much less emphasised now, and you could well be willing to go without almost anything in the drive to get what you really want from life.

14 FRIDAY *Moon Age Day 22 Moon Sign Leo*

You now have what it takes to be at the forefront of the action, a position you really enjoy! Conforming to expectations might not be easy, so for most of the time today you may not even bother to do so. With less emphasis on home and family than for most of November so far, you continue the month with a social flourish.

15 SATURDAY *Moon Age Day 23 Moon Sign Leo*

There now seems to be a strong accent on physical pleasures, though that doesn't mean you should slacken your efforts with regard to work. Loving relationships are quite obvious as places of resort once the working day is over, though you can't expect all those close to you to behave in a completely predictable way.

16 SUNDAY *Moon Age Day 24 Moon Sign Virgo*

This is a Sunday, and so it wouldn't be surprising if you were to choose to stay in the bosom of your family. Part of your nature will relish this, though it won't fully dispel any burning desire you have to address issues that are tricky to resolve at the weekend. Try to be patient and enjoy family times.

17 MONDAY *Moon Age Day 25 Moon Sign Virgo*

The accent today is on gathering news and information that is relevant to personal aspirations and wishes. With a great deal of joy on offer, you have everything you need to push forward towards specific horizons with energy and enthusiasm. In terms of personal happiness, this could be one of the best days of the month.

18 TUESDAY *Moon Age Day 26 Moon Sign Libra*

With the arrival of the lunar low, personal success is not well marked for the next few days and your best approach is to show a degree of patience. Conforming to the expectations of others shouldn't be difficult at present, and as long as you are not attempting to get ahead a great deal, this time can be quite comfortable.

19 WEDNESDAY *Moon Age Day 27 Moon Sign Libra*

Slowing down the action continues to be the order of the day. The lunar low does little for your energy levels, and under these circumstances you may find it difficult to see the road ahead quite as clearly as you would wish. Why not sit back and wait? Present trends don't last long, and do at least allow some time to rest.

20 THURSDAY *Moon Age Day 28 Moon Sign Libra*

Another day during which success may be elusive, yet a time during which personal attachments can offer a great deal. You would be wise to read the small print very carefully before signing anything today. A particularly scrupulous approach in business dealings can make all the difference during the current interlude.

21 FRIDAY *Moon Age Day 29 Moon Sign Scorpio*

Information you can glean from others today could prove to be both interesting and useful, so it is worthwhile keeping your ear to the ground. This is especially true in any situation regarding work. Conforming to expectations in personal matters could be difficult, especially if you feel your freedom is at stake.

22 SATURDAY *Moon Age Day 0 Moon Sign Scorpio*

Even if working too hard at the moment doesn't appeal, that shouldn't prevent you from getting ahead. With a tremendous ability to persuade others to put in the effort, you should find making progress a piece of cake. New partnerships are possible around now, especially ones of a business nature.

23 SUNDAY *Moon Age Day 1 Moon Sign Sagittarius*

If you manage to stay well in tune with the people who share your life in a social sense, you should be able to increase your popularity still further around now. This is a Sunday that would benefit from a change of scene of some sort. Aries soon gets bored if it is tied to the same place for days on end.

24 MONDAY *Moon Age Day 2 Moon Sign Sagittarius*

It's natural to feel frustrated if there are all sorts of little jobs that need dealing with today. The focus is on your desire to be up and away, but mundane aspects of life keep calling you back. Nevertheless, it's important to pay attention to what you are supposed to be doing, in order to avoid making too many silly mistakes.

25 TUESDAY *Moon Age Day 3 Moon Sign Capricorn*

In terms of your career, ask yourself whether your current plan of action is yielding the right results. Rather than abandoning it, perhaps you need to look at things afresh and make some modifications. Although goals and ambitions seem a long way off, with a little patience you can start an important personal journey.

26 WEDNESDAY *Moon Age Day 4 Moon Sign Capricorn*

You are definitely in the market for interesting conversation at the moment. However, trends encourage you to check and recheck your actions today, especially at work. Creating a positive impression counts for a great deal just now. Just be careful that the nervous side of the Aries character doesn't take over!

27 THURSDAY *Moon Age Day 5 Moon Sign Aquarius*

Being decisive is one thing, but whether those close to you are willing to make their own decisions is another. You can't live other people's lives for them, though you may be able to exert a significant influence at this stage. Personal confidence is present in great measure, especially in situations where you are selling yourself.

28 FRIDAY *Moon Age Day 6 Moon Sign Aquarius*

Excellent results come from practical efforts, and you have scope to make all sorts of forward movement in your life. Getting through a great deal of work shouldn't be hard, but bear in mind that social trends are good too, heightening a definite desire to please yourself. Don't be too keen to follow expected routines.

29 SATURDAY *Moon Age Day 7 Moon Sign Pisces*

Your powers of attraction have rarely been more emphasised, so much so that you might even be attracting your own fan club at this time! Although it pleases you to be liked, things can become slightly uncomfortable if people dote on you too much. There is much to be said for showing that you have your faults and failings too.

30 SUNDAY *Moon Age Day 8 Moon Sign Pisces*

The more you mix today, the greater is the buzz you can get from life generally. If there is a job you have been shying away from recently, why not get it out of the way once and for all? Most Aries people should already be planning for a week that can offer scope for lots of excitement and the chance of financial progress.

♈

December

2014

1 MONDAY *Moon Age Day 9 Moon Sign Pisces*

Once again there is potential for plenty of admiration of various types. Some of it comes from you and is directed towards those with whom you feel a great affinity. But it works in both directions, so don't be surprised if you find yourself part of a mutual appreciation society at the start of this working week.

2 TUESDAY *Moon Age Day 10 Moon Sign Aries*

The arrival of the lunar high encourages you to stick to doing what is important to you personally. If others try to talk you out of it, remember that they have their own agendas. By all means compromise over family matters, while at the same time keeping to your own agenda in the more practical areas of life.

3 WEDNESDAY *Moon Age Day 11 Moon Sign Aries*

Once you have Lady Luck on your side you can afford to push your ideas forward in a very progressive way. This would be an ideal time to communicate with those who haven't featured in your life for a while. There could be some interesting news about and this offers a chance to get ahead in the professional stakes.

4 THURSDAY *Moon Age Day 12 Moon Sign Taurus*

The charming side of your nature is highlighted today, and you need to ensure that this fact is not lost on those around you. If you have to work today, you have what it takes to bring a degree of happiness to those around you, while at home you should be able to inspire almost anyone, but especially younger people.

5 FRIDAY *Moon Age Day 13 Moon Sign Taurus*

Today is about finding things in your life that will make you feel generally happy and contented with your lot. There's nothing wrong with temporarily shelving your accustomed need to get ahead at all costs, in favour of sitting back and relaxing. It should offer an opportunity to survey your accomplishments so far this year.

6 SATURDAY *Moon Age Day 14 Moon Sign Gemini*

Do keep your life as varied as you can and don't be too tied to issues that are of no real importance. There are gains to be made by cherry-picking at present, opting for those aspects of life that have a genuine fascination for you. Any confusion arising in social or travel arrangements is best resolved sooner rather than later.

7 SUNDAY *Moon Age Day 15 Moon Sign Gemini*

Influences relating to career matters are much to the fore. This might involve little things you hear that encourage you to look carefully at half-forgotten matters or ones that didn't look important before. Intuition counts for a great deal, and ought to tell you when a potential purchase is really worth the asking price.

8 MONDAY *Moon Age Day 16 Moon Sign Cancer*

This would be a good day for putting new projects into action. Take full advantage of the input of those around you. Unusual characters in particular could have a specific part to play in your thinking and planning. A sea change of attitude becomes possible, and could lead you down paths that were previously unthinkable.

9 TUESDAY *Moon Age Day 17 Moon Sign Cancer*

Financial challenges are par for the course at the moment and they need to be addressed very carefully. Even if you have been taking certain matters for granted, that probably won't work right now. Caution is the keyword, something that is often difficult for your zodiac sign to address.

10 WEDNESDAY *Moon Age Day 18 Moon Sign Cancer*

A day to bring domestic matters into focus, even if this means ignoring some of the more practical issues of life for a while. Christmas is just around the corner and you won't get away with shelving the issue. Conforming to the patterns others set for you may well be easier than would normally be the case.

11 THURSDAY *Moon Age Day 19 Moon Sign Leo*

Places of entertainment have a great deal to offer now, which is probably just as well given the time of year and the season. It's sensible to think carefully about what you eat and drink, as overindulgence is not to be recommended. What definitely would be to your advantage is putting yourself in the social limelight.

12 FRIDAY *Moon Age Day 20 Moon Sign Leo*

Life becomes even more interesting and there is little time for circumspection. You can now afford to be very much a creature of the moment, and meditating probably won't be at the top of your agenda. Reacting in a moment-by-moment sense is what makes Aries tick, so such trends are no problem to you.

13 SATURDAY *Moon Age Day 21 Moon Sign Virgo*

Airing the way you feel can sometimes be uncomfortable if you are an Aries individual, though this would be a favourable time to do so. The position of the Moon offers an opportunity to spill the beans, which could be an emotional experience. In the end, though, it does allow you to give others a better understanding of you.

14 SUNDAY *Moon Age Day 22 Moon Sign Virgo*

There are signs that everyday obligations can now be a cause of some frustration. This situation can be mitigated if you allow others to take some of the strain. Delegating any facet of your life is not easy, but is a lesson worth learning because it prevents you from becoming too fatigued. Avoid family arguments like the plague!

15 MONDAY *Moon Age Day 23 Moon Sign Virgo*

Being an Aries subject, it might have only now finally sunk in that Christmas is just around the corner. Today would be an opportunity to make sure that all details are sorted out as quickly as possible, and the week ahead might include plans for an epic shopping spree. Make all arrangements as much fun as you can.

16 TUESDAY *Moon Age Day 24 Moon Sign Libra*

The lunar low encourages you to exercise a degree of caution when it comes to the practical aspects of life. This isn't made easier if you have a lot of demands upon your time at the moment. The spotlight is definitely on the social side of things, so be prepared to spread yourself very thinly!

17 WEDNESDAY *Moon Age Day 25 Moon Sign Libra*

Beware of taking anything for granted today. Your best approach is to check and double-check all arrangements. Does it seem that the lunar low is taking the wind out of your sails a little? If you are careful and circumspect, it needn't prevent you from dealing with your obligations or having some fun.

18 THURSDAY *Moon Age Day 26 Moon Sign Scorpio*

Freedom is the real key to happiness today. You need to take full advantage of a potentially upbeat and active period during which you should be showing your most positive face to the world at large. Allow your mind to explore, and make sure that the plans you are laying down for the weeks ahead reflect this process.

19 FRIDAY *Moon Age Day 27 Moon Sign Scorpio*

Mental stimulus can make all the difference now, so there is much to be said for tackling puzzles of one sort or another. These could be practical in nature, or simply for the sake of entertainment. There is also a focus on activity today, and on your desire to get as many Christmas preparations done as you can.

20 SATURDAY *Moon Age Day 28 Moon Sign Sagittarius*

A change of pace would do you the world of good around now. Why not leave work issues on the back burner for a couple of days and concentrate instead on what you can gain from your social life? This may not be the best time of all for starting a new health regime, but in the end only you can judge.

21 SUNDAY *Moon Age Day 29 Moon Sign Sagittarius*

If you are an Aries who is open to new romance, you may now have scope to turn a social contact into something much more. Others can consolidate personal attachments by finding moments to say those little words that are most important. Family-motivated interests are well starred this weekend.

22 MONDAY *Moon Age Day 0 Moon Sign Sagittarius*

With a potentially hectic period commencing both at home, and in particular at work, it may be difficult to find time for your own interests early this week. However, it's worth ensuring that you have at least a few moments every day for yourself, even if this means you have to put off one or two tasks until after the New Year.

23 TUESDAY *Moon Age Day 1 Moon Sign Capricorn*

Trends suggest there is something of the warrior about you at the moment, and it is unlikely that you would settle for second-best when it comes to defending those you love the most. Be prepared to deal with any arguments that result, using the power of your personality, which is emphasised now.

24 WEDNESDAY *Moon Age Day 2 Moon Sign Capricorn*

What really allows you to set today apart is your adaptable attitude and your willingness to learn as you go along. Christmas Eve offers opportunities for enjoyment, and the chance to gain an understanding of the true motivations and opinions of anyone who has been a closed book to you for some time.

25 THURSDAY *Moon Age Day 3 Moon Sign Aquarius*

A potentially high-spirited time, with the emphasis firmly on pleasure. All sorts of leisure-based opportunities are there for the taking, and you have everything you need to ensure you are the centre of attention. It's simply a matter of being in the right place at the right time, and presenting yourself as you are.

26 FRIDAY *Moon Age Day 4 Moon Sign Aquarius*

Look out for all the good things that are going on now, and for the chance to make connections with the sort of people you know are going to be useful to have around in the New Year. Beware of being too quick to jump to conclusions in personal attachments. It would be far better to ask a few leading questions.

27 SATURDAY *Moon Age Day 5 Moon Sign Pisces*

This is a favourable day for getting down to brass tacks generally and for letting others know the way you feel about certain issues. You can't expect everyone to agree with you, but when it matters the most you can get people on your side. Be ready to respond to opportunities to take on greater responsibility.

28 SUNDAY *Moon Age Day 6 Moon Sign Pisces*

Getting ahead today is very much about being in the know, which is why it's important to ask the right questions. Although present astrological trends encourage a focus on the practical considerations of life, this needn't prevent you from spending as much time as you can in and around your home.

29 MONDAY *Moon Age Day 7 Moon Sign Aries*

Once again, the lunar high emphasises your energy and general high spirits, and you have what it takes to show a confident face to the world at large. Be ready to offer support and advice to anyone who asks for it. This might even include a superior, so this is your time to show what you are made of and to shine at work.

30 TUESDAY *Moon Age Day 8 Moon Sign Aries*

This is an ideal chance to display the best side of the Aries nature, and to show others exactly what you have to offer. What you say and do today, especially at home, can set the seal on a number of events beyond New Year, so it's very important to put in that extra effort that can make all the difference.

31 WEDNESDAY *Moon Age Day 9 Moon Sign Taurus*

Talking to anyone shouldn't be a problem, even the sort of people who have not figured in your life before. By the evening, you can afford to get yourself into a definite party mood. There's plenty for Aries to look forward to, though tinkering with the nuts and bolts of personal attachments is not to be recommended.

ARIES:
2015 DIARY PAGES

ARIES:
YOUR YEAR IN BRIEF

The year may start in a rather confused way for Aries, but don't worry because it won't be long before you are back on form and turning things to your advantage. Some care is necessary at work and there might be times when you have to rely on the help and support of people you haven't taken to in the past. Romance looks fairly good and there are certainly likely to be some moments when your relationships are a good deal warmer than the seasonal winter weather.

Along comes the spring and a good deal of excitement is on the cards during March and April. You want to do all you can for those you love, but there are likely to be occasions when you simply have to tell people what you really think. Not everyone is going to be on your side in your professional life, but it is only a matter of time before your naturally dominant ways see you rising to the top again.

Keeping up with the pace of life might seem somewhat difficult at times during May and June, but in reality you are doing far better than you might imagine. People from the past may return to your life and could bring with them some happy memories, as well as sound advice to help you avoid repeating past mistakes. There are tedious jobs to be done which you won't relish, but the secret is to bite the bullet and to get them out of the way.

With the high summer comes the chance to be yourself and really get cracking on some of those jobs that have been waiting for a few months. July and August should find you on top form and anxious to make the best impression you can on the world at large. Just about everyone around you seems willing to lend a hand and there is no doubt that you will be at your best when it comes to sporting activities. Romance pays a repeat visit to your life.

September and October should find you slowing down a little. It isn't that you fail to get on well or to make a favourable impression, but you will take your time. At work you are confident and able to make the best impression by simply moving along steadily and you can consolidate on gains made when you were more up-front and go-getting. Keep your options open when it comes to travel.

Most Arians will want to end the year with a flourish, and there is plenty of opportunity to get ahead in both November and December. A little disorganisation can be expected at first, but it won't take you long to straighten things out, both for yourself and for others around you. Aim to make Christmas truly special for loved ones and also for friends who may have been going through a hard time. Love and laughter accompany the very end of the year.

January 2015

1 THURSDAY *Moon Age Day 11 Moon Sign Taurus*

At this time you show yourself to be a natural leader and should put in the effort to get others to follow you. Avoid arguing for your limitations, but at the same time try to find that humble quality in your nature that others respect. It's a fine line, because you also need to show how confident you can truly be.

2 FRIDAY *Moon Age Day 12 Moon Sign Gemini*

Influences surrounding friendships and group matters are likely to be uppermost in your mind around this time. Family commitments might seem to hold you back a little, but in the main you are getting on well with almost everyone. Of course there are bound to be exceptions, but that's the nature of life so try to take it in your stride.

3 SATURDAY *Moon Age Day 13 Moon Sign Gemini*

Make this a day of honesty – but only up to a certain point. There are a few people around who might not be up to facing the truth as you see it and for them it will be necessary to approach reality in easy stages. A little diplomacy can go a long way and may ensure you retain the popularity that is important to you.

4 SUNDAY *Moon Age Day 14 Moon Sign Gemini*

Be sure everyone understands what you are saying and why. This means being clear and concise in your communications, whilst at the same time going into detail if necessary. Don't get too tied down with the problems of others, except in those cases when you are sure you have the answers at your fingertips.

5 MONDAY *Moon Age Day 15 Moon Sign Cancer*

When it comes to meeting new people you are clearly in your element at the moment. At the same time you might find you are giving a good deal of energy to personal attachments. It may occur to you that things on the romantic front are growing a little samey and if so consider doing something to enliven this aspect of your life.

6 TUESDAY *Moon Age Day 16 Moon Sign Cancer*

Getting to where you want to be in life doesn't come without a significant amount of effort. As a rule you can be the hardest worker of all, but for now you may find you need to take a broad overview of life and aren't too keen on sticking to one theme throughout the whole day. From a social point of view, take advantage of opportunities to make new friends.

7 WEDNESDAY *Moon Age Day 17 Moon Sign Leo*

Your generosity knows no bounds today, though of course there is nothing unique about this fact because Aries at its best can be magnanimous and helpful. It doesn't really matter who is asking you for help, be ready with both advice and your practical skills. Be alert for a hint of the mysterious entering your life.

8 THURSDAY *Moon Age Day 18 Moon Sign Leo*

People who enter your life as newcomers might seem more than willing to trust you and give you the benefit of the doubt in most situations. Tomorrow might offer you the chance to make a few changes and to get away from routines, if you are willing to take the chance to do so. Friends are out for fun and clearly want to involve you.

9 FRIDAY *Moon Age Day 19 Moon Sign Virgo*

Do your best to slow down the pace of life today because it is likely that some issues are running away with you. This may not be the case in terms of romance, because things could hardly be working better for you in this sphere of your life. You know exactly what to say in order to sweep someone off his or her feet.

10 SATURDAY *Moon Age Day 20 Moon Sign Virgo*

Beware of too many emotional drives playing out in your life at the same time. You could be deeply attached to more than one individual, though there is probably also a great sense of responsibility involved. This could cloud your judgement. It is likely that you will come to the conclusion that something will have to be toned down.

11 SUNDAY *Moon Age Day 21 Moon Sign Virgo*

If you have to deal with slightly unpleasant confrontations today, it would be best to get these out of the way as early in the day as you can. At least that way you won't dwell on situations for too long and can then concentrate on more pleasant matters. Friends are likely to be getting in touch with you all through the day.

12 MONDAY *Moon Age Day 22 Moon Sign Libra*

It might be wise to avoid taking on new commitments today, unless you are sure you can see them through. One thing at once is the adage for Aries at present and even then you should concentrate to get things right. Even though you find it difficult, you may have to call upon the good offices of colleagues and friends.

13 TUESDAY *Moon Age Day 23 Moon Sign Libra*

It would be sensible to keep life as simple as you can today because you are now in that short period that comes along each month when the Moon occupies your opposite zodiac sign of Libra. This is known as the lunar low and is generally a time during which you need to recharge your batteries. Keep a low profile.

14 WEDNESDAY *Moon Age Day 24 Moon Sign Scorpio*

There should be time enough today to attend to everything you see as being important in a professional and practical sense, whilst at the same time having moments to spare that you can lavish on loved ones. When people need advice they are quite likely to turn to you at the moment – even if you have little experience in what ails them.

15 THURSDAY *Moon Age Day 25 Moon Sign Scorpio*

Don't hold back when people genuinely want to know what you think. Being diplomatic is likely to come quite naturally to you at this stage of the month. Romance could be on your mind and if you have been looking for a new love this could be the right time to concentrate your efforts.

16 FRIDAY *Moon Age Day 26 Moon Sign Scorpio*

You can't expect to get on with everyone and it is entirely possible today that one or two people are proving to be very difficult to deal with. If this turns out to be the case you would be well advised to avoid them altogether, in favour of individuals who give you no problems. Don't try too hard to change the world – just live in it.

17 SATURDAY *Moon Age Day 27 Moon Sign Sagittarius*

It is the strange nuances of life that are likely to captivate your imagination today. Keep an eye out for all sorts of bizarre coincidences or little happenings that you can't properly explain. Take note of them, because one or two of the situations that come about as a result could be turned to your distinct advantage later.

18 SUNDAY *Moon Age Day 28 Moon Sign Sagittarius*

If you play your cards right, this could be a delightful – and possibly surprising – Sunday. Make the most of feeling relaxed and confident and you'll find that almost everyone you meet will be happy to fall in line with your ideas. But don't overdo it and become arrogant, because even to Aries too much pride is not a good thing. Look to your friends for inspiration when you need it.

19 MONDAY *Moon Age Day 29 Moon Sign Capricorn*

If you seek out good company, this week could turn out to be a cracker from a social point of view. Take advantage of opportunities to mix business with pleasure, because it is possible that someone who has been little more than a colleague in the past will turn out to be very much more in the future.

20 TUESDAY *Moon Age Day 0 Moon Sign Capricorn*

You might not take too kindly to being given instructions at the moment, especially if the person handing them out has no real idea what he or she is talking about. There is a limit to your patience when you are dealing with those you see as less capable than yourself, but there are times when it would be better to count to ten than to lose your temper.

21 WEDNESDAY *Moon Age Day 1 Moon Sign Aquarius*

Personality clashes are more or less inevitable today because you are coming up against people who can be as stubborn as you. When an irresistible force meets an immovable object something has to give and it might have to be you. Avoid blank refusals when invitations come along, because you can benefit from the change.

22 THURSDAY ☿ *Moon Age Day 2 Moon Sign Aquarius*

Now you will have to think on your feet. Not all the answers you require will be around you all the time and your strong intuition comes into play. Speaking of playing, you are in the market for some fun and may also be quite competitive at the moment. You really do want to win and that means you try that much harder.

23 FRIDAY ☿ *Moon Age Day 3 Moon Sign Pisces*

Things are likely to be quieter for the next couple of days, mainly because the Moon is now going through your solar twelfth house. Don't get bogged down with details but instead focus on the broad overview of life most of the time. When you are not committed to work, take time out to relax.

24 SATURDAY ☿ *Moon Age Day 4 Moon Sign Pisces*

Some sort of outing might do you good today so why not make the most of any sales that are about because you could find you pick up a bargain or two. With everything to play for in terms of finances, it looks as though you could be slightly better off than you expected to be and you should keep an eye out for positive news relating to your finances.

25 SUNDAY ☿ *Moon Age Day 5 Moon Sign Aries*

Put your best foot forward and be willing to undertake anything that seems to be even remotely possible. Every one of your reactions is likely to be good and if you can't succeed at present, ask yourself if you could put in more effort. People from the past who emerge again could bring some surprises with them.

26 MONDAY ☿ *Moon Age Day 6 Moon Sign Aries*

When it comes to progress today, be guided by your feelings and intuitions. This is a decisive phase so you won't be waiting around for messages to come in; on the contrary your reactions are lightning quick. Even so, you are unlikely to put a foot wrong. Your competitive streak will be on display so make sure you are magnanimous should you lose – yes, that is possible.

27 TUESDAY ☿ *Moon Age Day 7 Moon Sign Taurus*

Listen and watch, and only react when you know the time is right. You will need to let others take some of the strain just now, whilst you recharge flagging batteries. Nobody can keep up the frenetic pace that you do indefinitely and it won't do you any harm at all to spend a few hours planning rather than doing.

28 WEDNESDAY ☿ *Moon Age Day 8 Moon Sign Taurus*

This may be the best time of the month to get new schemes up and running. You have had plenty of time to plan your strategies and now you should come out fighting. Of course, there could be occasions when you will defend yourself before you are attacked but you are able to say sorry when necessary and won't think yourself to be perfect.

29 THURSDAY ☿ *Moon Age Day 9 Moon Sign Gemini*

You are a positive inspiration to practically everyone who has a part to play in your day and you certainly give more to life than you take from it. This period has much to offer in terms of social happenings and instead of just being the life and soul of any party it should be you who is organising most of them.

30 FRIDAY ☿ *Moon Age Day 10 Moon Sign Gemini*

Don't be too quick to take offence today because the offhand remarks of others may not be directed at you. There is plenty of opportunity right now to shine in a social sense but only if you are willing to co-operate and become one of a team. Affairs of the heart could be proving slightly problematic but you can minimise that by treading carefully.

31 SATURDAY ☿ *Moon Age Day 11 Moon Sign Gemini*

Your practical qualities are important today and you'll pitch into anything new, knowing that you can cope well enough. This is laudable but do stop and think whether you should really be asking the advice and assistance of someone who can genuinely be considered an expert.

♈

February

2015

1 SUNDAY ☿ *Moon Age Day 12 Moon Sign Cancer*

Try to engage in projects that need to be finished before you look to take on new ones. If you complicate situations too much at the moment you are going to become bogged down and won't find success easy to achieve. Affairs of the heart should be going well. If you are not in a relationship, that may change very soon – be on the look out.

2 MONDAY ☿ *Moon Age Day 13 Moon Sign Cancer*

Your social life and group ventures should be working out extremely well, though there could be slightly less of a sense of satisfaction regarding family-based matters. It could be that you are failing to understand what it is that relatives really want of you. The problem is compounded if you sense that they don't really know either.

3 TUESDAY ☿ *Moon Age Day 14 Moon Sign Leo*

It may be a good thing to make a break with the past. At the same time you may be noticing for the first time this year that the days are lengthening, with a slight promise that spring is on the way. Today and until the weekend you would benefit from plenty of fresh air and the chance to fill your lungs somewhere beautiful. Get away if you can.

4 WEDNESDAY ☿ *Moon Age Day 15 Moon Sign Leo*

Make this a great day for communication, and not just in a verbal sense. Benefits can come from letters, emails or text messages. At the same time, keep up on what is happening in the area where you live. Being in touch with the world also means you will put yourself in the best possible position to make gains.

5 THURSDAY ☿ *Moon Age Day 16 Moon Sign Leo*

There is now an even more positive emphasis on communication so make the most of it and get out there and talk to people – you'll learn much. The astrological influences are shining on your talent for being persuasive and saying the right thing at the right time – make the most of it.

6 FRIDAY ☿ *Moon Age Day 17 Moon Sign Virgo*

This is a good time to co-operate, especially in plans that take you out of the ordinary and that prevent you from having to follow old or routine patterns of behaviour. Anything that gets you out of the house will be good on this particular Friday, so relish the chance to get to know new people in exciting places.

7 SATURDAY ☿ *Moon Age Day 18 Moon Sign Virgo*

This can be a fitting time to improve your personal life and may be the first time in days that you have the time to stop and notice your nearest and dearest. This can sometimes be a problem for Aries. It isn't that you fail to care, simply that your life becomes so busy you don't spend the time you might showing your affection.

8 SUNDAY ☿ *Moon Age Day 19 Moon Sign Libra*

You will probably notice today how difficult it is to keep up the sort of pace you have been happily maintaining for a couple of weeks. It would be best not to dwell on things today, but to jog along happily until things begin to gain pace once more. Today might find you in contemplative mood, but don't let that slide into being miserable.

9 MONDAY ☿ *Moon Age Day 20 Moon Sign Libra*

Although today may start out slowly and without a great deal of promise, by the time the afternoon arrives things are likely to look and feel somewhat different. Try to do something with your finances today – you could discover that something you did a while ago is only now starting to attract the attention you had hoped it would.

10 TUESDAY ☿ *Moon Age Day 21 Moon Sign Libra*

This is a good time to eliminate non-essentials and to push forward into uncharted but exciting territory. Aries is at its best right now and you certainly have what it takes to turn heads more or less wherever you go. On the social scene you should be especially lively so make sure you join in at every opportunity.

11 WEDNESDAY ☿ *Moon Age Day 22 Moon Sign Scorpio*

You are feeling real enthusiasm but make sure it is not misplaced. All the same you won't notice your little failures because so much is happening that will turn out to your advantage. The best advice would be to order your routines and do things one at a time, but it is advice that is likely to fall on deaf ears.

12 THURSDAY ☿ *Moon Age Day 23 Moon Sign Scorpio*

Many people find you an inspiring person to be with and this is a fact that is much enhanced by present planetary trends. They could hardly fail to notice your optimistic and sunny nature, which is quite often present in the case of Aries subjects. Impressing colleagues and superiors should be easy, so make the most of it.

13 FRIDAY ☿ *Moon Age Day 24 Moon Sign Sagittarius*

Certainly the potential for greater personal freedom is strong and most of the people you know will now seem to relish your ideas for reform and alteration. This is a fruitful period for travel and for all cultural matters. There is much pleasure to be had from being involved in stimulating conversations with intelligent people.

14 SATURDAY *Moon Age Day 25 Moon Sign Sagittarius*

You want to be a freewheeler today and to do whatever takes your fancy. Unfortunately the responsibilities of life are inclined to get in your way. Don't be put off by this because in an overall sense you are pushing forward and making significant headway. This would be a good day to go shopping.

15 SUNDAY *Moon Age Day 26 Moon Sign Capricorn*

You have the means to get on well, but could be slightly held back by the limitations that Sunday places upon you. The saying goes that you reap what you sow and you have been so busy spreading seeds around during the last two weeks that you should really be starting to notice how many benefits and gains are arising.

16 MONDAY *Moon Age Day 27 Moon Sign Capricorn*

Commitment is the key to success now and you should not be afraid to nail your colours to any mast that is important to you. There isn't much mileage in being half-hearted, particularly when it comes to work situations. Even if you sometimes make the wrong decisions, you will find ways and means to triumph anyway.

17 TUESDAY *Moon Age Day 28 Moon Sign Aquarius*

Avoid dwelling too much on personal issues and instead commit yourself to practical matters and to getting things done in and around your home. You probably won't be too inspired by the February weather and so will want to keep warm, so keep moving – and that could mean going out for a brisk run!

18 WEDNESDAY *Moon Age Day 29 Moon Sign Aquarius*

Don't waste your time and energies on superficial matters, but instead commit yourself to causes you know are going to be important for you in the future. Rules and regulations are apt to get on your nerves at this time, but you can find ways around these. You won't exactly break the rules, but you might bend them a little.

19 THURSDAY *Moon Age Day 0 Moon Sign Pisces*

Getting ahead now seems to be a matter of charm and Aries is not short of that commodity at present. In many ways you display yourself at your best to the world at large. Take care, though, that your pride doesn't get in the way today because you suspect that someone is trying to undermine your ideas or your authority.

20 FRIDAY *Moon Age Day 1 Moon Sign Pisces*

Relationships could now become the focus of your attention and though you might not reach any startling conclusions you are likely to be keen to make changes when you think they are necessary. For example, someone who has been little more than an acquaintance up to now could soon prove to be a loyal friend.

21 SATURDAY *Moon Age Day 2 Moon Sign Aries*

Today marks the start of the lunar high – that part of each month when the Moon returns to your own zodiac sign of Aries. Make the most of the burst of energy to get on with things and maximise your luck. The odd speculation could well pay off at this time, but don't take silly chances.

22 SUNDAY *Moon Age Day 3 Moon Sign Aries*

With everything to play for, this is one day during the month of February when you really do need to focus and to put in your best effort. As a reward, life will give you plenty of chances to get ahead so make sure you take them and grab your opportunities. You make your own luck so concentrate on what you are best at.

23 MONDAY *Moon Age Day 4 Moon Sign Aries*

You can now go all out for what you want and will be engaging in single-minded pursuits. If you take part in sport, you are much more likely to win today than to lose. For those Arians who are at work today, it is likely that people higher up the tree than you are will now be in a good position to help you out in some way.

24 TUESDAY *Moon Age Day 5 Moon Sign Taurus*

Close ties are positively cemented under present planetary trends and you show today just how loyal you can be. A good percentage of your time is likely to be spent supporting others and you are fair in your attitude to life generally. This is Aries at its best and you can be fairly certain that you are being noticed by all manner of people.

25 WEDNESDAY *Moon Age Day 6 Moon Sign Taurus*

Leisure and pleasure are pulling you in right now, which may dull your commitment to work. It's hard to concentrate on mundane matters when there is so much on offer personally and socially. Don't waste the opportunity – you can always catch up at a later date.

26 THURSDAY *Moon Age Day 7 Moon Sign Gemini*

If you are keen to get on with plans for the future, this could be a great time to go for it, but there is a note of caution in the planetary influences. Do check things out and be careful what you take on because Aries hates to be a laughing stock and you wouldn't want to discover that people are smirking at you behind your back.

27 FRIDAY *Moon Age Day 8 Moon Sign Gemini*

If there is one thing you seem to be looking for today it is security. Anything you can do to make yourself feel more comfortable and to bolster your financial resources for the future is grist to the mill at the moment. There are quieter times in store, so you do need to remain generally active today and to get things done quickly.

28 SATURDAY *Moon Age Day 9 Moon Sign Cancer*

Aries the perfectionist is on display this weekend and you are unlikely to embark on any project unless you are sure that you can see it through to a positive conclusion. The only slight problem is that you may spend so much time getting things right that you miss a few other opportunities that are waiting in the wings.

March

2015

1 SUNDAY *Moon Age Day 10 Moon Sign Cancer*

Don't be lulled into a false sense of security just because of what others are telling you. You have the potential to look at matters for yourself and to turn over a few stones, if necessary. You have your Sherlock Holmes hat on and though your attitude might amuse some of your friends, it could turn out to be worthwhile.

2 MONDAY *Moon Age Day 11 Moon Sign Leo*

Make the most of visits today to gather up new incentives and feed your imagination. Take advantage of any opportunity to move around at the moment and to avoid being stuck at home where nothing much is likely to be happening. You may have the opportunity to support someone who is important to you.

3 TUESDAY *Moon Age Day 12 Moon Sign Leo*

This is a time for renovations and for putting yourself to the test. It looks as though there are some cracking opportunities coming your way so don't be left at the starting post in a race for new possibilities. This is especially true when it comes to possible changes you want to make in and around your home.

4 WEDNESDAY *Moon Age Day 13 Moon Sign Leo*

There is plenty of energy around at the moment, so use some of it to seek out new friends and involve yourself in different activities. What you are unlikely to be doing is tying yourself down with ever more oppressive living or working conditions. Freedom is your keyword for the future now.

5 THURSDAY *Moon Age Day 14 Moon Sign Virgo*

New personalities are likely to be entering your life at any time now and that should make for an interested and varied social life. Those closest to you can be a little difficult to deal with and this is most likely to be the case with younger family members. Fortunately, you remain calm.

6 FRIDAY *Moon Age Day 15 Moon Sign Virgo*

Look out for people you don't get to see all that often and, if the mood takes you, seek out those you haven't met at all for a number of years. Of course, they will seem to have grown far older than you have and that fact at least will please you! Many of the comments you make at the moment are likely to be deliberately tongue in cheek.

7 SATURDAY *Moon Age Day 16 Moon Sign Libra*

Drop the reins of control for a few hours and let others work on your behalf. Meanwhile, seek out interesting ways and means of entertaining yourself, just as long as whatever you choose doesn't demand a great deal of energy. Get in touch with friends later in the day and think about an evening of quiet fun.

8 SUNDAY *Moon Age Day 17 Moon Sign Libra*

You might be forgiven for believing that a good deal of what is happening around you at present is very low key. This is the gift of the lunar low, which is inclined to take the wind out of your sails somewhat. If you find that people around are less than helpful, it might be best to abandon something, at least for the moment.

9 MONDAY *Moon Age Day 18 Moon Sign Libra*

You seem to have a natural talent for communicating this month and your ability to get your message across in any given situation knows no bounds. Find new ways to enjoy even the most tedious tasks, and jobs that normally take you a while to complete will be finished in a flash. Friends will be a great help.

10 TUESDAY *Moon Age Day 19 Moon Sign Scorpio*

You remain very active and especially courageous as a new week really gets started. In fact you are in just the right frame of mind to start new projects and to make them work for you from the very beginning. Romance may well feature strongly in your thinking and you could be looking for ways to really impress someone you fancy.

11 WEDNESDAY *Moon Age Day 20 Moon Sign Scorpio*

The emphasis at the moment is on your ego. More than one planetary position shows that you need to feel important and to be certain that others appreciate the effort you might put in on their behalf. This isn't really a problem, but there could be occasions when you become just a little too demanding and too self-seeking.

12 THURSDAY *Moon Age Day 21 Moon Sign Sagittarius*

There are matters around today that will tax your patience, but you should prove yourself to be equal to them. Although you can sometimes get very frustrated if things don't go the way you want, for the moment stay relaxed and prepare to wait. Your greatest virtue at the moment is your generosity.

13 FRIDAY *Moon Age Day 22 Moon Sign Sagittarius*

The progress you make now appears to have no limits but beware because things could grind to a definite halt if you push too hard. For this reason it would be best to finish what you start today, so that you can move ahead with the feeling that there is nothing crucial that remains outstanding. Arrange for a relaxing evening.

14 SATURDAY *Moon Age Day 23 Moon Sign Sagittarius*

Help comes from some fairly surprising directions today, even though you are probably unwilling to accept some of it. Just remember that everyone has their story to tell, even people you don't care for all that much. In fact, be prepared to accept that you might have been wrong in your appraisal of a particular individual.

15 SUNDAY *Moon Age Day 24 Moon Sign Capricorn*

You can approach a variety of interests at the moment and will be quite happy doing anything that takes your fancy. Don't expect to be concentrating too much on any one particular task, because you browse rather than concentrate under present trends. You should also discover that you are more romantically inclined than you thought.

16 MONDAY *Moon Age Day 25 Moon Sign Capricorn*

Domestic matters go with a swing and you may already be planning for events that are intended for next weekend. If you can't get everything you want at the moment in a financial sense, try to console yourself with the fact that you are doing most things right and that dividends will come along eventually.

17 TUESDAY *Moon Age Day 26 Moon Sign Aquarius*

There should be plenty of interesting things going on socially so get out there and enjoy yourself. Today offers variety, though most of what happens depends on your own input. Don't wait around for others to make the running. Instead, simply pitch in and it is likely that others will follow your lead.

18 WEDNESDAY *Moon Age Day 27 Moon Sign Aquarius*

You have a great imagination at the moment and many ideas should be popping into your head. You can't possibly follow up on all of them, but a couple of departures might be good. Most of all you need to feel interested in your life and may have to work extra hard in order to get things going your way.

19 THURSDAY *Moon Age Day 28 Moon Sign Pisces*

A pretty low-key period is present while the Moon occupies your solar twelfth house. There isn't likely to be anything bad happening; it's simply that you can't get up the speed of efficiency you would wish. The lunar high is just around the corner, so you should prepare for busy times to come.

20 FRIDAY *Moon Age Day 0 Moon Sign Pisces*

There is still much to be gained from privacy and solo pursuits, and you will make greater gains if you stay out there in the public eye. There's a bit of a conflict here because the Moon is still in your solar twelfth house. By tomorrow, all of that becomes a thing of a past, so maybe you should be getting ready.

21 SATURDAY *Moon Age Day 1 Moon Sign Aries*

This ought to be a very successful time for Aries. If it isn't, consider working harder. Life offers you new incentives and all you really have to do is to accept them when they come along. Making gains at the moment is a little like picking fruit and Lady Luck is likely to play a part in your day.

22 SUNDAY *Moon Age Day 2 Moon Sign Aries*

As is often the case, you are more than willing to accept the accolades that come your way, but you do so in such a pleasant and magnanimous way that nobody begrudges you your successes. You might not think of yourself as being a generally lucky individual, but a great deal seems to be going your way just at the moment.

23 MONDAY *Moon Age Day 3 Moon Sign Taurus*

Personal relationships are now likely to be a favoured area on which to concentrate. If you feel you haven't made much fuss of your partner or sweetheart in the recent past, now is the time to put things right. A timely gift or even a few well-chosen words would be appreciated and could bring a response you might not expect.

24 TUESDAY *Moon Age Day 4 Moon Sign Taurus*

Your strength of character is now challenged by slightly difficult circumstances. If this turns out to be the case you have the chance to show what you are really made of. Aries keeps going when others fall by the wayside and your approach to life is all-important. In a few days' time, most things are likely to look more positive.

25 WEDNESDAY *Moon Age Day 5 Moon Sign Gemini*

Emotions are still rather up and down and on this particular day there's a danger that you won't be pushing yourself as hard as you know you should. Don't fall into that trap, even if you feel a certain degree of frustration. Very soon you will have the opportunity to do whatever takes your fancy, but for the moment you will probably have to follow the wishes of others.

26 THURSDAY *Moon Age Day 6 Moon Sign Gemini*

This is definitely a day to get ahead by taking action. This period of high ambition coincides with planetary help to line things up in the way you would wish them to be. One by one you hit most of your targets and might even be surprised at your own ability to change circumstances for the better. Avoid unnecessary routines today.

27 FRIDAY *Moon Age Day 7 Moon Sign Cancer*

Compromise could prove to be quite beneficial today. You are likely to achieve most when you are willing to listen to another's point of view. Don't be too keen to get your own way with loved ones. If you listen very carefully, you could discover that someone close to you has a wisdom well beyond their years.

28 SATURDAY *Moon Age Day 8 Moon Sign Cancer*

There might be very little time for fulfilling your own personal desires today, mainly because you are working so hard on behalf of others. There could be something of a conflict between your ego and the need to make compromises, some of which feel unnecessary. Use your intuition as the best possible guide now.

29 SUNDAY *Moon Age Day 9 Moon Sign Cancer*

Keep your plans simple and you can't really go wrong. The only time you are like to stumble at the moment is when things get too complicated. Although as an Aries subject you are used to concentrating on a dozen different things at the same time, that kind of response to life is going to get you into slightly hot water for now.

30 MONDAY *Moon Age Day 10 Moon Sign Leo*

If you are feeling rather misunderstood today, it would be sensible to ask others to clarify their point of view and to be somewhat more considerate towards you. On the other hand, you could just as easily let things pass, because you are probably too sensitive for your own good. You may also feel rather tired at times today.

31 TUESDAY *Moon Age Day 11 Moon Sign Leo*

This is an important time to have a good understanding of what makes you tick on a subconscious level. A little meditation is in order, together with a period spent thinking about your true motivations in various areas of your life. The answers you come up with might surprise you, but the effort will have been well worthwhile.

April 2015

1 WEDNESDAY *Moon Age Day 12 Moon Sign Virgo*

There could be some scope for a few shortcuts to success at the moment, mainly because your attitude is so positive and people are happy to help you along. Whatever the request, don't be surprised if you find someone who is willing to lend a hand; and it's only fair, really, because you do a great deal for others day-to-day.

2 THURSDAY *Moon Age Day 13 Moon Sign Virgo*

Now you are more inclined to buckle down and to look more carefully and seriously at business interests. There are likely to be discussions regarding future security and maybe the possibility of a specific document to sign. Right now you can rely on your own good sense, as well as on some very specific and pointed advice.

3 FRIDAY *Moon Age Day 14 Moon Sign Virgo*

You bring a great sense of innovation to almost everything you do now and there isn't much doubt that you are very inventive and can come up with some particularly good ideas. Some of your notions could be turned to your advantage at a later date and it's worth salting away a few ideas, or even writing them down somewhere.

4 SATURDAY *Moon Age Day 15 Moon Sign Libra*

It is more or less inevitable today that things will slow down and that you will be unable to get everything you want from specific situations. It's a strange thing, but when life was hectic a few days ago you showed a great deal of patience. Now, when you really need it the most, you seem to have a great lack of that particular virtue.

5 SUNDAY *Moon Age Day 16 Moon Sign Libra*

The lunar low is still showing itself in almost every facet of your life and you seem to have little choice but to react to situations, rather than instigating them yourself. Don't worry, because in a day or so things are going to look very different. In the meantime, you are left with some fairly solitary moments that can also be beneficial.

6 MONDAY *Moon Age Day 17 Moon Sign Scorpio*

Don't get upset when it is necessary to make small alterations to your routines. These are likely because of changing family requirements, together with a probable restlessness on the part of your partner. Just go with the flow and enjoy what comes along today, whether you have decided upon it or not.

7 TUESDAY *Moon Age Day 18 Moon Sign Scorpio*

You are progressive and far-sighted at the moment and the only potential difficulty lies in getting others to recognise that your ideas make great sense. Recognise that while to you real opportunity lies in being able to react according to changing circumstances, to others habit is all-important.

8 WEDNESDAY *Moon Age Day 19 Moon Sign Scorpio*

Today is mostly about expressing yourself and it relies heavily on your ability and willingness to speak out for your own good. If this puts you into conflict with your partner or family members you can at least rely on your diplomacy, which is strong at present. Continue your efforts towards making necessary changes within your home.

9 THURSDAY *Moon Age Day 20 Moon Sign Sagittarius*

Recent practical trends continue, though you don't have to look too hard for answers at a time when you know instinctively how to act and to react. Not everyone will be on your side or will accept your point of view at face value, but that doesn't really matter. On the contrary it gives you the opportunity to sharpen your intellect.

10 FRIDAY *Moon Age Day 21 Moon Sign Sagittarius*

Life continues to work out fairly well for you, even if things do tend to quieten a little today. That may be no bad thing because you often keep up a pace that tires you and exhausts those with whom you interact. Finding time to stop and smell the flowers is sometimes very important, even to the ever-progressive and always busy Aries.

11 SATURDAY *Moon Age Day 22 Moon Sign Capricorn*

For those of you who are working Aries subjects, there is now a good chance that career prospects are looking especially good. There might not be a great deal you can do to help the situation on a Saturday, but you should have time to think about things and to plan your strategies for the week that lies ahead. Have some fun this evening.

12 SUNDAY *Moon Age Day 23 Moon Sign Capricorn*

The greatest benefits today come from the strange mixture of individuals who are presently playing a part in your life and your thinking. You might have to go back to square one in order to address one issue, but the effort would be worthwhile because you want to get something important sorted out once and for all.

13 MONDAY *Moon Age Day 24 Moon Sign Aquarius*

Make this a fulfilling time socially by reacting positively to invitations that are coming your way. You won't be so busy that you can't stop for a while and enjoy the positive social trends that are around. On the contrary, there are great gains to be made by those amongst you who are willing to mix business with pleasure.

14 TUESDAY *Moon Age Day 25 Moon Sign Aquarius*

Friendships have much going for them today and you might be quite willing to drop the traces of responsibility altogether in favour of simply enjoying yourself. A day out would suit you down to the ground. It doesn't much matter where you decide to go, because it is the change of scenery and the sense of excitement that counts.

15 WEDNESDAY *Moon Age Day 26 Moon Sign Pisces*

You will be very busy today and most of what you are doing involves communication in one way or another. In your heart you feel in the mood for a little luxury but there won't be enough time to cosset yourself, which could lead to a few frustrations. Simply blame a few sticky planetary positions and wait for a few days.

16 THURSDAY *Moon Age Day 27 Moon Sign Pisces*

Although there are likely to be disagreements in and around your home there is no reason why you should have to become involved. It would be far better today to keep your counsel unless you are specifically asked for an opinion. Even then it would be sensible to hold fire and not to tell it the way an Aries subject usually would.

17 FRIDAY *Moon Age Day 28 Moon Sign Aries*

Things are likely to speed up noticeably now as the Moon races into your own zodiac sign. This is certainly not a day to rest on your laurels and if you act quickly you can make significant gains. Some of these are likely to be financial in nature but it has to be said that the very best trends during this lunar high are romantic in nature.

18 SATURDAY *Moon Age Day 29 Moon Sign Aries*

You should be feeling at your very best now and will be dealing with what once looked like problems head on. In your present frame of mind there isn't much that is likely to get in your way and you have what it takes to impress most people. Put your luck to the test and be sure to recognise the green light when you see it.

19 SUNDAY *Moon Age Day 0 Moon Sign Taurus*

In terms of friendship there should be some very light-hearted moments to be enjoyed this Sunday. It looks as though you will be getting on extremely well with just about anyone you meet and this is just what you need at present. If there are a few people who insist on being miserable you will simply have to leave them to it.

20 MONDAY *Moon Age Day 1 Moon Sign Taurus*

You can assist yourself in your career at the moment by making the right sort of contacts. If you have been looking for advancement or even a new job, this could be one of the best times to keep your eyes open. Even the casual remarks made by colleagues and friends can start you thinking in radically new ways.

21 TUESDAY *Moon Age Day 2 Moon Sign Gemini*

It is towards the material aspects of life that your mind is apt to turn at this particular stage of the week. There is a subconscious need for you to feather your own nest at present and you won't be at all happy unless you feel yourself to be totally in control of your own finances. Getting others on side should not be difficult.

22 WEDNESDAY *Moon Age Day 3 Moon Sign Gemini*

There is now a readiness about you to find new solutions to old problems. This may manifest itself as considerable inventiveness and you will be more than happy to look again at situations you didn't deal with very well before. Routines can be something of a drag, because your mind is flirting most with originality and change.

23 THURSDAY *Moon Age Day 4 Moon Sign Gemini*

You could find yourself spending far more time at home than you anticipated, though there is no negativity about the trends that bring this possibility. On the contrary, it looks as though you will be quite happy with your lot and very anxious to please your partner and family members. If a celebration is at hand make a special fuss this time.

24 FRIDAY *Moon Age Day 5 Moon Sign Cancer*

Although you are willing to work long and hard to achieve your desires, you might be feeling that you should be succeeding more than seems to be the case. This is probably because you are getting restless and impatient again. The trouble with Aries is that it wants everything now – and usually has what it takes to get it.

25 SATURDAY *Moon Age Day 6 Moon Sign Cancer*

You show a great sense of practicality when dealing with the routines of today, but don't forget this is the weekend and that you need to let those around you know that you are available to spend some time with them. Your own personal interests might have to be put on the back burner for a short while, but the delay will be worthwhile.

26 SUNDAY *Moon Age Day 7 Moon Sign Leo*

Your powers of discrimination are not up to scratch, so you need to be especially careful in all your dealings today. If there is a chance of financial speculation you would be well advised to put this aside until well into the new week. This is a good period to retrench and to look again at all matters before committing yourself.

27 MONDAY *Moon Age Day 8 Moon Sign Leo*

A hardworking drive for success could lead to improved financial prospects at this time. With Mercury in a strong position, not only are you communicating well, but also you can be sure that others are really listening to what you have to say. Economic ingenuity and fresh ideas are what set this period apart.

28 TUESDAY *Moon Age Day 9 Moon Sign Leo*

It isn't difficult for Aries people to appreciate the good things in life, which can include excellent food and drink, as well as an elevated social scene. You can have all of this at present, but what you can't expect to do is to burn the candle at both ends indefinitely. A little rest may be called for and you will have to accept it.

29 WEDNESDAY *Moon Age Day 10 Moon Sign Virgo*

Your natural faith in the principle of abundance will be reflected in your material success around now. It looks as though Aries is now willing to spend money in order to make money, even if one or two people raise an eyebrow at your intentions. In the end it seems that you have to follow your own motivations and intuition.

30 THURSDAY *Moon Age Day 11 Moon Sign Virgo*

Your superior way of dealing with people on a personal level is likely to stand you in good stead at the end of this month. Almost anyone will enjoy meeting you at the moment because you are so interesting and have such a lot to say. The only word that could be used to describe your nature adequately at present is 'charismatic'.

May
2015

1 FRIDAY *Moon Age Day 12 Moon Sign Libra*

There could be a tendency towards low energy and a general lack of excitement in your life for the next couple of days, and for this you can blame the lunar low. Even so, that doesn't mean to say that life will lack any sort of pleasure. On the contrary, as long as you opt for fairly quiet activities you could be very happy indeed.

2 SATURDAY *Moon Age Day 13 Moon Sign Libra*

With the lunar low comes a slight downturn in the general quality of your life. It looks as though you will have to be more careful in your dealings with others, particularly at home, and you won't have the level of energy that was around a few days ago. Stick to routines if you want to make at least some progress.

3 SUNDAY *Moon Age Day 14 Moon Sign Libra*

Look out for promising financial initiatives today and don't turn down the chance to make a pound or two you had not been expecting. There are possible professional gains around at the moment, too, and you should be very good when it comes to recognising an opportunity that comes on a plate.

4 MONDAY *Moon Age Day 15 Moon Sign Scorpio*

Loved ones seem to be doing everything they can to be pleasant and to make life easier for you. Although there might not be anything especially exciting about today it does have its own gentle rewards, most of which come from the direction of your partner or friends you really rate.

5 TUESDAY *Moon Age Day 16 Moon Sign Scorpio*

Confine yourself today to what you know best. There isn't any real point in trying to break new ground and you can get on better if you consolidate present positions. Although you are likely to encounter some really awkward people around this time, you manage to deal with them quite successfully.

6 WEDNESDAY *Moon Age Day 17 Moon Sign Sagittarius*

Cut any losses immediately and push ahead on all fronts. There is no point in dwelling on matters that are over; only a positive view of the future is going to help you. Look for social occasions that might present the opportunity for the enjoyment you need in life, but for today try to avoid mixing business with pleasure.

7 THURSDAY *Moon Age Day 18 Moon Sign Sagittarius*

Keep your ears open today, because even the most casual conversations can carry news that will be of use to you in the days ahead. You are not usually one for gossip so you could ignore something detrimental you hear about a friend and that is the best way forward. Avoid unnecessary details in financial transactions.

8 FRIDAY *Moon Age Day 19 Moon Sign Capricorn*

Try for a varied and interesting social life and, if necessary, relax some of the pressure you have been putting upon yourself in more practical ways. It seems as though you will have to be just a little careful in your handling of colleagues, some of who are so touchy you can barely speak to them today.

9 SATURDAY *Moon Age Day 20 Moon Sign Capricorn*

The potential for success at work is especially strong under present planetary trends, but this will not be of much use to you unless you work at the weekend. Either way you prove to be optimistic and well able to get on top of small problems. At home you might discover something to your advantage.

10 SUNDAY *Moon Age Day 21 Moon Sign Aquarius*

Look towards the assistance that comes your way from both family members and friends. If you insist on doing everything yourself today there probably will not be time for the personal enjoyment that is also on offer. You could discover that something you have been dreading disappears like the morning mist.

11 MONDAY *Moon Age Day 22 Moon Sign Aquarius*

It isn't surprising that your mind is turning towards hearth and home around now, because there are several planetary trends that point in that direction. At the same time you may harbour a burning desire for change and this can set up some confusion in your head. Try to compartmentalise your life as much as possible.

12 TUESDAY *Moon Age Day 23 Moon Sign Aquarius*

With less of a commitment to personal matters right now and a greater desire to feather your nest in some way, it appears that you are turning your attention towards necessary changes, most likely in your working routines. If you are between jobs, use today to concentrate your efforts.

13 WEDNESDAY *Moon Age Day 24 Moon Sign Pisces*

It looks as though romance is in the air for many Aries people out here in the middle of the week and at least some of the attention coming your way could be from fairly surprising directions. Don't be too quick to believe something you hear in the news or from a colleague until you have had the time to mull it over.

14 THURSDAY *Moon Age Day 25 Moon Sign Pisces*

Keep talking, because that is the best way to make friends and influence people. Your sunny and warm disposition keeps you popular and brings new possibilities, even when you are dealing with people you hardly know. The rewards for simply being the open and interested person you naturally are can be significant.

15 FRIDAY *Moon Age Day 26 Moon Sign Aries*

Now is the time for action. Forget some of the inhibitions and difficulties of the last few days, and instead commit yourself to situations and be willing to push your luck. There are agencies around on which you can rely and if there is something you really need, all you have to do at the moment is ask.

16 SATURDAY *Moon Age Day 27 Moon Sign Aries*

Another potentially terrific day is in store. This is a good day to push forward on several different fronts, with energy and the will to succeed. You may even be able to sort out a troublesome situation that has been around for weeks or months. Romance has rarely been better than it seems to be at the moment.

17 SUNDAY *Moon Age Day 28 Moon Sign Taurus*

On the social front, you are likely to be very much in demand at the moment. There is plenty to keep you occupied right now, even if at first you don't make quite the progress you might wish in all practical senses. This should be a good day for romance, especially for the young or young at heart.

18 MONDAY *Moon Age Day 0 Moon Sign Taurus*

There is likely to be a significant boost to friendships and deeper relationships, thanks in part to the present position of the Moon in your solar chart. You are likely to be mixing freely with a number of newcomers in your life and can be assured of making the most favourable sort of impression when it matters most.

19 TUESDAY ☿ *Moon Age Day 1 Moon Sign Gemini*

There is a genuine need at the moment for relaxation from pressuring situations and that means making a conscious decision not to get too involved in certain matters. Allow others to take some of the strain whilst you sit back and delegate. This isn't easy for Aries, but occasionally it is necessary.

20 WEDNESDAY ☿ *Moon Age Day 2 Moon Sign Gemini*

You probably come across as being extremely interesting and quite funny. General trends increase your wit and make it easy for you to bring people in on your many fascinating conversations. Don't try to rush your fences and remember that you will get what you want with patience and determination.

21 THURSDAY ☿ *Moon Age Day 3 Moon Sign Cancer*

Getting your own way shouldn't be difficult today and you are likely to be forcing a few issues if those around you seem unwilling to act of their own accord. Working steadily towards your most cherished objectives, you force just about anyone to recognise how organised and capable you are.

22 FRIDAY ☿ *Moon Age Day 4 Moon Sign Cancer*

You are still communicating successfully with colleagues and friends, though it is important also to find a balance in your attachments to family members. One of two people to whom you are close could be acting in a somewhat strange manner. Your job for today is to find out why this should be the case.

23 SATURDAY ☿ *Moon Age Day 5 Moon Sign Leo*

Your own sense of independence is what drives you along noticeably right now and though this is a very positive thing, it can cause certain problems in your associations with those around you. It's worth taking on board the fact that not everyone's nature works in quite the way yours does.

24 SUNDAY ☿ *Moon Age Day 6 Moon Sign Leo*

A fairly progressive phase continues and you can make this Sunday your own by taking some notion that has been floating around in your head for a while and making it into a reality. Someone you don't see very often could be appearing in your life again and might bring a little potential excitement with them.

25 MONDAY ☿ *Moon Age Day 7 Moon Sign Leo*

You should see benefits coming along both at work and later when you are in the bosom of your family. There is a good balance in your nature at the moment between things that are practical and those that are purely personal in nature. Getting to grips with a wayward family member should be easy now.

26 TUESDAY ☿ *Moon Age Day 8 Moon Sign Virgo*

The emphasis at the moment is definitely with home and family, even if this is not a situation that seems to be of your own choosing. The fact is that people have very definite needs of you at this time and you will have to be on hand to offer all the help and support that proves to be so crucial during this period.

27 WEDNESDAY ☿ *Moon Age Day 9 Moon Sign Virgo*

Try to make something big happen today. It doesn't really matter what part of your life is in the spotlight. What's important is to leave everyone around you feeling what a tremendous person you are and how much they would like to follow your lead. Popularity isn't difficult to find.

28 THURSDAY ☿ *Moon Age Day 10 Moon Sign Libra*

Put what seem like crucial decisions on the back burner and realise that everything will come right in its own good time. You can't rush anything whilst the lunar low is about and will only cause yourself extra and unnecessary anxiety by trying to push yourself too hard. People should be pleased to lend a hand.

29 FRIDAY ☿ *Moon Age Day 11 Moon Sign Libra*

Making money can be something of a struggle today, probably simply because there appears to be more going out than is coming in. Be patient, because the trends later are better. The lunar low really kicks in now and causes you to falter over matters that seemed easy to deal with before.

30 SATURDAY ☿ *Moon Age Day 12 Moon Sign Libra*

There are now major changes in store as far as your practical life is concerned. The slight worry caused by the lunar low is out of the way and the real driving quality of your nature returns. Personal attachments in particular look good and you should be able to find exactly the right words to impress your lover.

31 SUNDAY ☿ *Moon Age Day 13 Moon Sign Scorpio*

This looks like a time during which you will visit the past in some way. This could have something to do with home-based issues that seem to be uppermost in your mind right now. Don't get so preoccupied with things that are over that you forget your commitment to what is happening right now.

2015

1 MONDAY ☿ *Moon Age Day 14 Moon Sign Scorpio*

A better day for business and a time during which you ought to be willing to take the odd chance in order to get others to take note of your strategies and opinions. You won't be at the back of any queue when it comes to getting your message across, but not everyone can be expected to show the same enthusiasm as you do.

2 TUESDAY ☿ *Moon Age Day 15 Moon Sign Sagittarius*

Fate seems to be ready to lend a helping hand when it matters the most. Just when you think you are stuck for an idea, something happens that sets you back on the path to gain. From a social point of view it might seem more like a weekend than a Tuesday and this is particularly true in the evening.

3 WEDNESDAY ☿ *Moon Age Day 16 Moon Sign Sagittarius*

There seems to be a strong focus on work today and a great desire to break down barriers that once got in your way. You are approaching life in the way a good Aries person should and show great optimism when it matters the most. Look out for a romantic period later in the day that should lift your spirits.

4 THURSDAY ☿ *Moon Age Day 17 Moon Sign Sagittarius*

Although you might be rather shocked by the attitude being taken by loved ones, in the end you will probably have to admit that they are right and will fall in line with their thinking. This could be an unusual day, with personal lessons coming in from a number of different directions and in surprising ways.

5 FRIDAY ☿ *Moon Age Day 18 Moon Sign Capricorn*

A very adventurous sort of Aries subject is on display at this time and in a social sense at least the weekend starts here for many of you. Look for something very different to do and don't worry if certain other people disapprove. The fact is that you need to follow your own motivations under present planetary trends.

6 SATURDAY ☿ *Moon Age Day 19 Moon Sign Capricorn*

Stand by for a period of distinctly high spirits and a time during which you tend to be very mischievous. This could be one of the funniest interludes of the month and represents a time during which you will be keen to display all the humour that sits at the heart of the average Aries nature.

7 SUNDAY ☿ *Moon Age Day 20 Moon Sign Aquarius*

There is a strong urge beginning to stir within you to break out of restrictions and to get on with your life in more positive ways. This is the sort of situation that comes so naturally to your sign, there isn't much that you can do except follow your own lead. However, there are still gains to be made from quiet moments.

8 MONDAY ☿ *Moon Age Day 21 Moon Sign Aquarius*

Beware of acting a little like a prima donna today if you can't get what you want from life. There's nothing too peculiar about this state of affairs, bearing in mind your Sun sign. However, to recognise the fact and to laugh at yourself is the best way to deal with such an inclination.

9 TUESDAY ☿ *Moon Age Day 22 Moon Sign Pisces*

You should be fully in gear today when it comes to dealing with the practicalities of life, and especially anything to do with work. Give a thought to the needs and wants of friends and don't allow yourself to be held back by the negative considerations of people who just thrive on being miserable.

10 WEDNESDAY ☿ *Moon Age Day 23 Moon Sign Pisces*

A slightly quieter day comes along ahead of the lunar high, which begins tomorrow. It's time to clear the decks for action because there is likely to be no stopping you once tomorrow arrives. Take a little time out to get to know certain people better – even those you think you understand well enough already.

11 THURSDAY ☿ *Moon Age Day 24 Moon Sign Aries*

Personalities of one sort or another will be entering your life at all stages today and this applies as much at work as it does in your home life. With everything to play for, show a very happy face to the world and from a romantic point of view you should be at your most seductive. Others are certain to notice.

12 FRIDAY ☿ *Moon Age Day 25 Moon Sign Aries*

With energy now definitely at a peak you are in the most potentially successful time of the month. Be bold and brash because for the moment you can get away with it. Take the most important of your schemes and put them into practice. Socially speaking, life should be looking especially good.

13 SATURDAY *Moon Age Day 26 Moon Sign Taurus*

The social scene is inclined to offer a few surprises now the working week is out of the way for most of you. Information gathering is presently well starred, as are all romantic attachments and communication associated with love. Personalities tend to predominate in your life at present and you are clearly one of them.

14 SUNDAY *Moon Age Day 27 Moon Sign Taurus*

Although there can be a marked sense of upheaval in your personal life, it appears that it can be mostly put down to your present point of view. Don't view little upsets as being of any real importance and avoid arguing about matters that are of no real significance. Vary things socially and avoid being with one individual too much.

15 MONDAY *Moon Age Day 28 Moon Sign Gemini*

Your mind functions clearly and those around you appear to be falling in line much more readily than has been the case for the last few days. Romance is emphasised by present trends and words of love are easy to impart, especially for those who are in settled relationships. New love can be slightly more difficult to control.

16 TUESDAY *Moon Age Day 29 Moon Sign Gemini*

You should be in for a fairly good time on the domestic front. There are some gains to be made at work, but these could be limited in scope and you might be better off concentrating your efforts where they are going to work best. Relatives should be especially co-operative, even those who are generally awkward.

17 WEDNESDAY *Moon Age Day 0 Moon Sign Cancer*

Extended communication is worth a look, because there could be some gains to be made through keeping in contact with people who are far away across the world. Considerable effort needs to be put into new plans, because it is becoming obvious that they won't mature without your intervention.

18 THURSDAY *Moon Age Day 1 Moon Sign Cancer*

Your charming nature and optimistic outlook seem more obvious to others today than they probably will to you. You can now act almost entirely on instinct and shouldn't be tardy when it comes to making instant interventions. This is particularly the case in group situations.

19 FRIDAY *Moon Age Day 2 Moon Sign Cancer*

Meetings that have to do with business should be working out very well for you around this time. Aries subjects who are involved in education will probably discover around now that they are doing rather better than they expected. Even so, don't leave details to chance and especially not ones that have a bearing on your social life.

20 SATURDAY *Moon Age Day 3 Moon Sign Leo*

The time is right to try something new and unusual. Mars is in a strong position and offers a unique and dynamic approach to new situations. Considering the ideas and opinions of others is important because they may have notions that haven't occurred to you, but these could offer some real rewards.

21 SUNDAY *Moon Age Day 4 Moon Sign Leo*

You can expect good support from family members and won't be easily fazed by anything today. The planetary line-up is particularly good for you around this time, because it brings you a combination of sensitivity and action. It might be said that Aries is working at its very best under present circumstances.

22 MONDAY *Moon Age Day 5 Moon Sign Virgo*

Put various creative thoughts into words and don't settle for second-best, either from yourself or others. You may have to lay down the law a little, especially if you are in a position of some authority. Keep an open mind about the problems of a friend and don't let that newly discovered sensitivity slip.

23 TUESDAY *Moon Age Day 6 Moon Sign Virgo*

A boost to work developments is on the cards, even if you have done nothing yourself to bring it about. Today is all about making the most of any opportunity that comes along and is not a time during which you can afford to look any gift horse in the mouth. A family member could be depending on you.

24 WEDNESDAY *Moon Age Day 7 Moon Sign Virgo*

This is a time during which you need to think about getting on with something simpler. By the end of today the Moon moves into your opposite zodiac sign, bringing the lunar low period. It's important to realise that this need not be a bad time, but simply a period when regeneration is called for.

25 THURSDAY *Moon Age Day 8 Moon Sign Libra*

Energy is in short supply and you need to be willing to let others do things for you unless you want your recent progress to slow. You might not be able to achieve much yourself, but there is scope for you to watch whilst others toil on. It's only fair because for most of the time it's you who does the majority of the work.

26 FRIDAY *Moon Age Day 9 Moon Sign Libra*

This is a good time to concentrate on domestic issues and to sort out one or two little problems that could be cropping up at home. Relatives are likely to be easygoing and will probably follow your lead far more willingly than might sometimes be the case. Best of all today, you are feeling far more confident.

27 SATURDAY *Moon Age Day 10 Moon Sign Scorpio*

Along comes a time of the month during which you want to widen your interests in some way and a period during which you can get on with a new project that is close to your heart. Meanwhile, you should also find yourself in a very romantic frame of mind and will know how to utter those most important words of love.

28 SUNDAY *Moon Age Day 11 Moon Sign Scorpio*

This would be a good time to look at all sorts of career projects, even though on a Sunday it is possible that you can't do anything about them in a practical sense. Don't argue for your limitations, because if you do there is a possibility that things will start to go wrong in unnecessary ways.

29 MONDAY *Moon Age Day 12 Moon Sign Scorpio*

There may be less time and inclination to chase social rainbows at the start of the week. A better plan would be to get some practical jobs out of the way and then to get some rest when you are not busy. Moments spent on your own could prove to be quite rewarding around this time.

30 TUESDAY *Moon Age Day 13 Moon Sign Sagittarius*

You should find that there are some good ideas around at present and not all of them are yours. It doesn't really matter where a notion comes from, just as long as you can turn it to your advantage. Give and take is important where your love life is concerned and especially so by this evening.

July 2015

1 WEDNESDAY *Moon Age Day 14 Moon Sign Sagittarius*

Look out for opportunities that allow you to enjoy yourself in specific ways. These probably don't include staying too close to home. It would be good to spend time in the company of people who stimulate the more intellectual side of your nature, maybe visiting historical or cultural centres of one sort or another.

2 THURSDAY *Moon Age Day 15 Moon Sign Capricorn*

If you have been jumping about from foot to foot because of a decision that has to be addressed, make up your mind today. People tend to listen to what you have to say and won't be judgemental or critical. What is more, you appear to be full of confidence and that inspires a positive attitude in others.

3 FRIDAY *Moon Age Day 16 Moon Sign Capricorn*

Not only should today begin a period that is more hectic from a social point of view, it also finds you far more confident when approaching matters that are not routine in your life. Gradually it becomes possible for you to influence all manner of people, some of whom are going to play an important part in your future.

4 SATURDAY *Moon Age Day 17 Moon Sign Aquarius*

This is a period when you are looking closely at life's finite situations. In other words, nothing lasts forever and you need to lay down plans for new ventures. That's something that is generally quite easy for Aries to do, but your skills in this direction are fine-tuned at the present time.

5 SUNDAY *Moon Age Day 18 Moon Sign Aquarius*

Personal relationships have much to offer at this part of the weekend, even though you may be busy in other ways, at least during the first part of today. It's well worth letting your nearest and dearest know how you feel about them and on the way you can offer tremendous support when it is needed the most.

6 MONDAY *Moon Age Day 19 Moon Sign Pisces*

If you are a working Aries, this is a time when you can put in that extra bit of effort that is going to make all the difference. Although you might be biting off more than you can chew in some departments, in terms of your social life everything should be working out just fine. This should be a stimulating Monday.

7 TUESDAY *Moon Age Day 20 Moon Sign Pisces*

This should be a good day, socially speaking. Where you have had some domestic problems, even outsiders can help to pour oil on troubled waters. Be willing to lend an ear to a friend who is having some sort of difficulty in his or her life. An awkward job should be coming to an end at any time now.

8 WEDNESDAY *Moon Age Day 21 Moon Sign Aries*

You arrive at the middle of the working week under the influence of the lunar high, so it's all stops out and full steam ahead. Where you come across obstacles, you now tend to push them aside in favour of radical moves and instant decisions. Things won't take long to do today, and there is plenty of support when you need it the most.

9 THURSDAY *Moon Age Day 22 Moon Sign Aries*

Keep up your efforts, because there is everything to play for today and no lack of incentive to get on with the positive aspects of life. Lady Luck seems to be on your side and you have what it takes to change circumstances to suit your own needs. This is not a time to be taking no for an answer.

10 FRIDAY *Moon Age Day 23 Moon Sign Taurus*

Romance and personal relationships should prove to be more than harmonious now and it is in the sphere of attachments that you gain most from today. Your partner might be making some heavy demands of you, though you probably won't care too much about that. Ring the changes socially.

11 SATURDAY *Moon Age Day 24 Moon Sign Taurus*

You can be extremely persuasive today and should have very little difficulty convincing others to follow your lead. This can be very useful if you work at the weekend and an advancement of some sort may be in the offing. The world tends to be pretty much as you make it right now, so think big.

12 SUNDAY *Moon Age Day 25 Moon Sign Taurus*

If there is something missing today, it's up to you to find what it is and put it right. For the moment you become a great lover of mystery and so won't mind delving a little into certain aspects of life. In terms of entertainment you are at a very flexible stage, though you do need to pep up your life as much as possible.

13 MONDAY *Moon Age Day 26 Moon Sign Gemini*

Compromise is not only advisable today, but also absolutely necessary. It won't always be easy to see a point of view you basically don't understand, but it's only a matter of time before explanations are forthcoming. Be prepared for things to happen that simply cannot involve you for the moment.

14 TUESDAY *Moon Age Day 27 Moon Sign Gemini*

Money-wise you may be getting things together better than has been possible at any stage for the last couple of months. Although you probably can't afford to spread cash around too much, you will be able to spoil someone you love and maybe gain something from the situation yourself.

15 WEDNESDAY *Moon Age Day 28 Moon Sign Cancer*

Social matters continue to be one of the most important facets of life as the week reaches its halfway stage. Although probably quite busy – which, let's face it, isn't unusual for you – it is possible to gain from quiet moments too. Being away from the rush and push of life can allow much-needed reflection.

16 THURSDAY *Moon Age Day 0 Moon Sign Cancer*

You are quite assertive today and for this reason alone others are not inclined to fall out with you. Give and take is important in matters of love, as is taking the time to talk to people who really need your support. You'll have to spread yourself fairly thinly to get everything done, but that won't be a problem for you.

17 FRIDAY *Moon Age Day 1 Moon Sign Leo*

There could be a good deal of support available, and at a time when it matters the most. Since this could be coming from just about any direction it's important to keep your eyes open. Even casual conversations can lead to some important outcomes and will bring you closer to your heart's desire.

18 SATURDAY *Moon Age Day 2 Moon Sign Leo*

Hearth and home represent the perfect setting for you at the moment. Although you may feel tied down by professional considerations, you are likely to get the most from domestic issues. Concentrate on loved ones and family matters to take your mind away from things you simply cannot resolve.

19 SUNDAY *Moon Age Day 3 Moon Sign Leo*

On a material level, you may find that others are more than considerate and supportive of your needs. There are some gains to be made today, though these are likely to come from rather unexpected directions. Keep in touch with colleagues at a distance who might be in a position to help you out in some way.

20 MONDAY *Moon Age Day 4 Moon Sign Virgo*

A happy-go-lucky attitude works best for you around this time and you should not take any aspect of life too seriously. Concentrate on issues that are close to your heart and spend time with loved ones. Your partner might have something special to tell you and it's very important to listen carefully.

21 TUESDAY *Moon Age Day 5 Moon Sign Virgo*

Now is the time to be enjoying social visits of one sort or another and it's likely that work takes second place to simply having a good time. That's fine because even Aries people can't be on the go all the time. Routines are somewhat tedious and, if possible, you will want to leave them to others.

22 WEDNESDAY *Moon Age Day 6 Moon Sign Libra*

Energy levels are somewhat depleted, so this is probably not the day to be climbing a mountain or shooting any rapids. In the main you will probably be quite content simply to wait and see, something you are particularly good at for the moment. Supportive people fill your life, which brings its own rewards.

23 THURSDAY *Moon Age Day 7 Moon Sign Libra*

Today might bring the realisation that holiday time is just around the corner. That will cause you a smile and make you walk in a jauntier manner. This part of the week should be yours to do with as you wish. Spend some time with family members, but some equally interesting moments with friends.

24 FRIDAY *Moon Age Day 8 Moon Sign Libra*

This would be a good time to engage in social activities, though it is true that you are probably also more committed to work matters than seemed to be the case earlier this week. There are some gains to be made that come out of the blue, so it's important to keep paying attention.

25 SATURDAY *Moon Age Day 9 Moon Sign Scorpio*

Your mind is filled with ideas at the moment and if there is any frustration about at all it comes from not being able to put all of them into operation. People should be generally helpful, but you won't be at all willing to accept their practical assistance or their advice if you suspect they have some agenda.

26 SUNDAY *Moon Age Day 10 Moon Sign Scorpio*

There can be a little luck about now with regard to your career. It probably won't be much, but enough to say you are being noticed and that others do have your best interests at heart. Meanwhile you are likely to be doing rather better in the romantic stakes.

27 MONDAY *Moon Age Day 11 Moon Sign Sagittarius*

You can make the most of a clear and inquisitive mind at present. Under present trends, discussing matters with others is of prime importance and you can afford to take the time out to explain yourself fully. As far as your personal life is concerned, things could be going better than you expected.

28 TUESDAY *Moon Age Day 12 Moon Sign Sagittarius*

You can turn both personal and professional matters to your own advantage and now find yourself sitting under a number of very positive planetary influences. Don't be too quick to settle for a compromise when in discussion with workmates. Chances are that you can do better and so you must stick to your guns.

29 WEDNESDAY *Moon Age Day 13 Moon Sign Capricorn*

Friendships can prove to be most beneficial and rewarding around this time. Your popularity and powers of attraction are both off the scale and you need to do whatever you can to make the most of these positive trends. You certainly should not sit in a corner and mind your own business, because it's time to be noticed.

30 THURSDAY *Moon Age Day 14 Moon Sign Capricorn*

Right now you can make the very most of both personal and professional aims. Almost anything you have in your mind can be attained under present planetary trends and you also enjoy a high degree of popularity with some important people. Strike while the iron is hot in terms of professional matters.

31 FRIDAY *Moon Age Day 15 Moon Sign Aquarius*

Take a hard look at financial aspects of your life, and you might discover that this is the time to put on the brakes where specific expenditure is concerned. It may be better to lose out a little in the short term than to find matters even more difficult later. It might be wise to avoid pointless speculation of any sort for the moment.

♈

August 2015

1 SATURDAY *Moon Age Day 16 Moon Sign Aquarius*

As a new month dawns you might have to look rather carefully at finances. It's possible that you have either been spending rather lavishly or else demands have been coming in from a number of different directions. Take time out to think in a professional sense and plan your strategies steadily.

2 SUNDAY *Moon Age Day 17 Moon Sign Pisces*

Home and family are under the planetary spotlight today as you find yourself making gains in all areas of life that are personal and even private. The deeper side of your nature is definitely in evidence, but this won't prevent you from continuing to enjoy yourself; it's just that now you are doing so in quite different ways.

3 MONDAY *Moon Age Day 18 Moon Sign Pisces*

A great deal of energy is likely to be put into your work today and there won't be all that much time for personal enjoyment. This is mainly because you are insistent on getting as much as possible done right at the start of the week. Although you can achieve a lot today it might be better to pace yourself just a little.

4 TUESDAY *Moon Age Day 19 Moon Sign Aries*

Your sense of direction is absolutely clear at the moment and you are unfettered by pointless worries about possible consequences. It might even be suggested that you are very calculating under the influence of the lunar high, but this is no problem either, particularly since you are working towards the success of others as well as yourself.

5 WEDNESDAY *Moon Age Day 20 Moon Sign Aries*

Good things are definitely likely to be happening to you today and you can enjoy this part of August in the knowledge that most of what you want is going your way. With more than your fair share of good luck, it looks as though you will be quite happy to take a few chances of a financial rather than a personal nature.

6 THURSDAY *Moon Age Day 21 Moon Sign Aries*

You are now in a period when it ought to be very easy to gather the information you need in order to get on better in a general sense. Your curiosity is roused and you will leave nothing to chance. Because you have so much energy, even the most insignificant details fall under your scrutiny and that means greater advancement.

7 FRIDAY *Moon Age Day 22 Moon Sign Taurus*

There are fresh ideas about and you have a great desire to push the bounds of the possible in any way you can. Today marks one of those periods when you could feel slightly tied down by convention and you will be determined to get away somehow. This could be a holiday, but even a day or two away from routines would be welcome.

8 SATURDAY *Moon Age Day 23 Moon Sign Taurus*

Although your workload could seem rather heavy, you undertake almost everything with a smile in your heart and a tune in your voice. This is clearly noticed by others and you should find that your influence with the world at large is greater than ever. This is achieved by simply being the person you naturally are.

9 SUNDAY *Moon Age Day 24 Moon Sign Gemini*

When it comes to achieving your objectives, today couldn't really be better. At work you show yourself to be more than capable of coming up with new ideas and there is a strong chance that some sort of advancement will be coming your way. At the very least your versatility is being noticed and that stands you in good stead generally.

10 MONDAY *Moon Age Day 25 Moon Sign Gemini*

With an even greater sense of movement and freedom, you will not be all that keen to be stuck in one place right now. On the contrary, you want to move about as much as possible, even if circumstances make this somewhat difficult. You are nothing if not ingenious and can find ways to have the best of all worlds at present.

11 TUESDAY *Moon Age Day 26 Moon Sign Cancer*

There are many light-hearted times to be had in a social sense, with new friends to be made and a consolidation of the affection you feel for people who are always around you. If you don't feel contented at the moment you may not be trying hard enough, though it has to be said that Aries is always searching and perpetually on the move.

12 WEDNESDAY *Moon Age Day 27 Moon Sign Cancer*

Impressing others with your good ideas won't be difficult, but beware because if you are throwing everything into the ring at the moment you are likely to have as many less-than-inspired notions as brilliant ones. The job you have to do is to determine which of your inspirations are likely to do you some good in the longer term.

13 THURSDAY *Moon Age Day 28 Moon Sign Leo*

This is a time during which there is plenty of romantic energy about. It doesn't matter whether you are eighteen or eighty, you will still feel the pull of deep affection and the need to express your feelings. You are also very much on stage at present and have a desire to find the right audience under differing circumstances.

14 FRIDAY *Moon Age Day 29 Moon Sign Leo*

It looks as though you will be demonstrating a great insight into the way others are behaving and this is especially true as far as your friends are concerned. You won't judge anyone, but will simply be in a good position to offer either the right advice or practical help when it matters the most.

15 SATURDAY *Moon Age Day 0 Moon Sign Leo*

In practical discussions today you show yourself to be quick-witted, funny and engaging. At home things are likely to be a little fraught, though probably not as a result of any circumstance created by you. Younger people especially can be a cause of some minor frustration and need dealing with carefully.

16 SUNDAY *Moon Age Day 1 Moon Sign Virgo*

The spotlight is on handling bigger responsibilities at this time, so make the most of opportunities to demonstrate that you are willing to stretch the bounds of the credible in order to prove yourself to others. Actually, you probably won't have to, because all you have shown yourself to be in the recent past will be enough.

17 MONDAY *Moon Age Day 2 Moon Sign Virgo*

Your ability to see both sides of almost any situation is quite noteworthy around now and you are subject to fairly inspirational ideas when it matters the most. Today should prove to be entertaining and filled with promise for those Aries subjects who are able to grasp new situations quickly.

18 TUESDAY *Moon Age Day 3 Moon Sign Libra*

The progressive phase that you have noticed of late is now more or less certain to slacken for a day or two. For this state of affairs you can thank the lunar low. There is little you can do about the situation except to accept that there are times when it is better to look ahead and plan than actually to get on with things.

19 WEDNESDAY *Moon Age Day 4 Moon Sign Libra*

This won't be the best day of the month for many Aries subjects, but neither is it likely to be as potent or difficult as the lunar low sometimes turns out to be. Keep it quiet and steady for today and tomorrow, doing those things that feed your intellect more than your pocket. This is a thinking time and has the potential to be a very potent one, if you are careful.

20 THURSDAY *Moon Age Day 5 Moon Sign Libra*

Things slump a little as you find yourself beset with a few practical problems, and maybe have no real way to sort them out immediately. Patience is called for – plus the assistance of someone who is clearly in the know. Don't be too inclined to assume that anything has been done correctly. It is important for you to check.

21 FRIDAY *Moon Age Day 6 Moon Sign Scorpio*

On the ideas front, you probably need to be careful about moving ahead too quickly. Test things out carefully and don't put too much effort in any direction unless you know that you will turn a profit of some sort. This doesn't apply to your personal life, of course, but even here you need to exercise a little care.

22 SATURDAY *Moon Age Day 7 Moon Sign Scorpio*

This ought to be a favourable period for all domestic issues and for making family business livelier and more rewarding. Let others have their head to a greater extent than might sometimes be the case. Even if your trust is slightly misplaced, it is necessary to allow younger people especially to find their own way in life.

23 SUNDAY *Moon Age Day 8 Moon Sign Sagittarius*

An important relationship may come fully into focus today. There could be some tension when it comes to making compromises, mainly because you are not in the right frame of mind to do so. Keep up your efforts to streamline your social life, or you could tire yourself out completely.

24 MONDAY *Moon Age Day 9 Moon Sign Sagittarius*

You are now in a lighter, brighter mood and won't mind in the least if someone seems to be questioning your way of doing things. You show great patience and make an excellent teacher at the moment, whilst still pushing steadily towards your own objectives. Family members can be a real source of joy at present.

25 TUESDAY *Moon Age Day 10 Moon Sign Sagittarius*

You may find yourself enjoying a little romance today and there is a definite chance of an emotional release. Some of the gains you receive around now come like a bolt from the blue, but you are naturally quick on the uptake and won't turn down any chance of a lucky break. All the same, this is not a good time for gambling.

26 WEDNESDAY *Moon Age Day 11 Moon Sign Capricorn*

You appear to the world at large to be very much at ease right now and indeed that is the truth. You show a good attitude when dealing with others and will not be stuck for an idea all day. This would be a great time to take a break away. If you are already on holiday, stand by to have what surely must be an excellent time.

27 THURSDAY *Moon Age Day 12 Moon Sign Capricorn*

There could be something rather irritating to do and if this is the case you would be well advised to get it out of the way as early in the day as proves to be possible. It is likely that a change of attitude is called for when it comes to dealing with a strictly practical matter. You might also have to eat a little humble pie, which isn't easy.

28 FRIDAY *Moon Age Day 13 Moon Sign Aquarius*

An easier day at work should find everything running quite smoothly, leaving you to please yourself to a much greater extent. New diversions are a possibility and you might be looking for some alterations to your social life, in order to allow time for new interests. This is not a day when you are likely to run out of steam quickly.

29 SATURDAY *Moon Age Day 14 Moon Sign Aquarius*

Work issues are likely to be boosted (although of course this won't be significant to Aries subjects who either don't work or who are away from work at the weekends). You are still anxious to have a good time and to show your best possible face in social situations. Don't be surprised if you are extra popular at present.

30 SUNDAY *Moon Age Day 15 Moon Sign Pisces*

You can work wonders today when it comes to simply communicating with others. Finding the right words to express yourself is rarely difficult, but it might be suggested that you are positively inspirational at the moment. Someone you see quite rarely might be making a repeat appearance to your life very soon.

31 MONDAY *Moon Age Day 16 Moon Sign Pisces*

A slightly quieter day could be coming along and this is thanks to the position of the Moon just ahead of the lunar high. Confidence is bubbling away below the surface, and this is a favourable time to think and plan ahead. Your mind is a maelstrom of possibilities, even if on the surface you appear to be cool and calm.

September 2015

1 TUESDAY *Moon Age Day 17 Moon Sign Aries*

There is no such thing as a sense of proportion whilst the lunar high is around. Today and tomorrow are such days and mark the time during September when you will be at your most dynamic and potentially successful. Lady Luck is clearly on your side at the moment and you can afford to take the odd chance.

2 WEDNESDAY *Moon Age Day 18 Moon Sign Aries*

You are now much more certain of your opinions and so the full potential of the lunar high is available to you. Don't wait to be asked today, because it is very important to take the initiative in most matters. Do your best to spur on romance and don't be too surprised by some of the attention that is coming your way.

3 THURSDAY *Moon Age Day 19 Moon Sign Taurus*

Though hectic from a social point of view, life can be very rewarding for Aries subjects at this time. You are in touch with whatever is going on in your vicinity and should be feeling that you have your finger on an important pulse. The attitude of younger family members may need to be addressed.

4 FRIDAY *Moon Age Day 20 Moon Sign Taurus*

This is an excellent time to get involved in new studies or in educational matters generally. There is a whole world to discover out there, a fact that is only now beginning to occur to you. Your curiosity is roused at every turn and Aries becomes quite the detective right now. Beware of friends acting in a mysterious manner.

5 SATURDAY *Moon Age Day 21 Moon Sign Gemini*

The domestic atmosphere is likely to become livelier today, offering you all sorts of incentives at home that haven't shown themselves of late. There should be much communication passing back and forth, together with the feeling that younger family members especially are making better progress now.

6 SUNDAY *Moon Age Day 22 Moon Sign Gemini*

Family encounters bring out the best in you at this time, in a period that is excellent for discussing personal matters of any sort. Plans related to home and the way you view it are of great importance so take your time over making decisions. Acting on impulse is far less likely today than has been the case recently.

7 MONDAY *Moon Age Day 23 Moon Sign Cancer*

Be on the alert for one or two hiccups in financial arrangements. These are not likely to be particularly important, but it is essential that you keep your eye on the ball in all financial transactions. It might be difficult to make yourself as available as you would wish in some situations.

8 TUESDAY *Moon Age Day 24 Moon Sign Cancer*

Whilst your main urge is to help as much as possible, at the same time there are plenty of things that need doing and only a limited amount of time available. Tuesday should mean spending time with relatives and friends, at the same time managing to ignore some of the practical necessities of life, at least for today.

9 WEDNESDAY *Moon Age Day 25 Moon Sign Cancer*

Happy social or even romantic events could be on the cards for today. Venus is in a good position at present, offering good prospects in terms of love and affection generally. On a more practical footing, you may have to watch out for someone who isn't doing things the way you had anticipated or wished.

10 THURSDAY *Moon Age Day 26 Moon Sign Leo*

Having fun should be your number one priority at present and there ought to be plenty of people around who will be more than happy to join in. Refuse to rise to the bait from someone who loves causing trouble. You are in a very generous mood at the moment and nothing is too much trouble when it comes to pleasing others.

11 FRIDAY *Moon Age Day 27 Moon Sign Leo*

You should not expect to be perpetually the centre of attention today. Actually it probably would be good to drop out of the limelight, at least for a few hours. There is plenty to be done behind the scenes and there are gains to be made from simply spending some time with loved ones.

12 SATURDAY *Moon Age Day 28 Moon Sign Virgo*

Your popularity rating seems almost certain to take a turn for the better any time now. As a result you can expect a fairly busy and quite successful sort of day. Where new tasks are concerned, it's important to start as you mean to go on. Friendship is possible with people you haven't seen eye to eye with in the past.

13 SUNDAY *Moon Age Day 0 Moon Sign Virgo*

Distractions are more or less inevitable today and although these could prove to be somewhat frustrating, it really all depends on your point of view. With nothing too important to achieve and plenty of moments when you can simply look at life, don't be in too much of a rush to reach all your objectives.

14 MONDAY *Moon Age Day 1 Moon Sign Virgo*

Don't make any significant decisions on a whim. There is time to think today, as well as to seek out some sound advice from people who are in the know. If you are involved in research of any kind, this would be a good period to intensify your search. Aspects of the past could prove to be important but nostalgia is out.

15 TUESDAY *Moon Age Day 2 Moon Sign Libra*

The lunar low is inclined to take the wind out of your sails and can prevent you from making the progress that seems second nature to you. There are ways forward, not least by allowing others to do some of the work and even to take the lead. The difficulty for you lies in letting go of the traces for a day or two.

16 WEDNESDAY *Moon Age Day 3 Moon Sign Libra*

You may be slightly happier with your lot today and will be getting used to the fact that you are in a quiet interlude about which you can do very little. Aries is definitely dreamier at the moment and can make much out of emotional and romantic encounters. Your mind is inclined to inhabit the past rather too much.

17 THURSDAY *Moon Age Day 4 Moon Sign Scorpio*

In terms of your skill to communicate with others it looks as though your personality is especially appealing today to those around you. This is not a time to hold back when it comes to your own opinions, particularly since you are in a good position to put them across without finding too many objections cropping up.

18 FRIDAY ☿ *Moon Age Day 5 Moon Sign Scorpio*

You can appear to be all things to all people under present astrological trends and the slightly harder and more caustic side of Aries has definitely taken a holiday. Because of your charm this is the time to get what you want, and you manage to do so in such a way that your requests sound like compliments.

19 SATURDAY ☿ *Moon Age Day 6 Moon Sign Scorpio*

You are very supportive of the ideas of those around you and this is especially true when it comes to family members and friends who have been present for years. Life is two-way traffic for the sign of Aries right now because you learn as much as you teach – a fact that is not lost on those you deal with the most.

20 SUNDAY ☿ *Moon Age Day 7 Moon Sign Sagittarius*

A boost to your love life is possible this Sunday, mainly because you find yourself with the time necessary to concentrate on this specific area of your life. Set out to have some fun and make sure that you include your partner. You may find you don't have to say very much because your attitude is very evident.

21 MONDAY ☿ *Moon Age Day 8 Moon Sign Sagittarius*

This period is especially favourable for most sorts of relationships, so the time is right for establishing a better rapport with someone who hasn't been your flavour of the month in the past. Whether you like them more or not remains to be seen, but what matters is that you are in a position to form some sort of understanding.

22 TUESDAY ☿ *Moon Age Day 9 Moon Sign Capricorn*

Although one or two of your ideas are a little impractical at the moment, you do have charm on your side, as well as an ability to exploit the potential you see in others. Don't be too quick to judge a colleague who may actually be seeing the future somewhat more sensibly than you are.

23 WEDNESDAY ☿ *Moon Age Day 10 Moon Sign Capricorn*

There is information around at this time that could turn out to be of significant use to you. Building on platforms you have created earlier you are able to modify your ideas and to react according to circumstances. Aries is shrewd and calculating under present planetary trends and that spells potential success.

24 THURSDAY ☿ *Moon Age Day 11 Moon Sign Aquarius*

Relating to others intellectually has never been easier than you will find it to be today. There is an ability to instinctively adopt the right attitude to get on with the prickliest of individuals and you discover that some people are willing to do almost anything just for the chance to make you smile.

25 FRIDAY ☿ *Moon Age Day 12 Moon Sign Aquarius*

A time of plain sailing is likely in terms of personal attachments and you shouldn't have to work very hard to impress anyone. Although you can be quite impulsive at present, many of your projects are for the sake of others. What people notice most about you under prevailing astrological trends is your generosity.

26 SATURDAY ☿ *Moon Age Day 13 Moon Sign Pisces*

Communal and social matters keep you pretty much on the go, from the moment you get out of bed until you crawl back into it again. Although this is a busy interlude it ought to be a very happy one, too, and represents a period during which fond memories are likely to be laid down for the future.

27 SUNDAY ☿ *Moon Age Day 14 Moon Sign Pisces*

This is a day during which you need to reflect and understand your own emotions. In particular you have to pay specific attention to the feelings of those around you. Aries is so busy that it sometimes fails to realise that it is treading on the toes of those individuals it relies upon the most. A few compliments are called for.

28 MONDAY ☿ *Moon Age Day 15 Moon Sign Aries*

Lady Luck is on your side and it is likely that you will be better off than you expected in a financial sense. The attitude of others is really not an issue because you are able to turn most situations around on your own. Play for high stakes and show people what Aries is truly capable of achieving.

29 TUESDAY ☿ *Moon Age Day 16 Moon Sign Aries*

Get an early start today because the planets are with you and there is plenty you can turn to your advantage. There are situations about now that require your personal touch if they are going to offer you what you want the most. The lunar high brings you both popularity and know-how.

30 WEDNESDAY ☿ *Moon Age Day 17 Moon Sign Taurus*

You could be seen by others as being just the right person to take charge of some project that requires a patient and practical approach. Advancement is on the cards for some sons and daughters of Mars and you show a very positive approach to almost any situation that comes your way.

October 2015

1 THURSDAY ☿ *Moon Age Day 18 Moon Sign Taurus*

There could be a few troublesome domestic issues to be sorted out at this stage of the week and that might mean getting behind in other matters. Exercise all the patience you can and simply do what seems most necessary. You can catch up later and in any case it comes down to being a matter of priorities in the end.

2 FRIDAY ☿ *Moon Age Day 19 Moon Sign Gemini*

Communication issues could run into difficulty if you don't keep on top of them. The basic reason is that others will misunderstand what you are trying to tell them and it is therefore very important that you double-check that messages are coming across as you intend. This is more likely to be an issue at work than in social settings.

3 SATURDAY ☿ *Moon Age Day 20 Moon Sign Gemini*

A good deal of adapting will be necessary at the moment if you want to get the very best out of life. For the last few days you have been under the influence of a few slightly awkward planetary influences and these could have left you feeling somewhat muddled. Today offers you the chance to think things through and to take action.

4 SUNDAY ☿ *Moon Age Day 21 Moon Sign Gemini*

Don't be bossy at home and allow family members to choose options for themselves. You don't mean to interfere, it's just your way but others may not be all that happy about the fact that you seem to know better than they do how to run their lives. If you listen and comment but avoid interference you can still have an input.

5 MONDAY ☿ *Moon Age Day 22 Moon Sign Cancer*

This could be one of the best times of the month for involving yourself in community issues and for getting to grips with a slight problem that has a bearing on just about everyone you know. You are very socially minded at the moment and the reforming tendencies of Aries show out strongly. You might even be quite political.

6 TUESDAY ☿ *Moon Age Day 23 Moon Sign Cancer*

Don't allow the views of others to influence your judgements to such an extent that you fail to address issues yourself. Aries might be just a little lazy at the moment and for that reason alone it will be easier to simply go with the flow. Force yourself to think about matters yourself and take whatever actions your mind suggests.

7 WEDNESDAY ☿ *Moon Age Day 24 Moon Sign Leo*

Your sensitivity is heightened and it looks as though you will be doing a great deal to support others today. There ought to be more time to address issues that are associated with your home life and family members will be pleased to have you around more. Your sunny and warm personality can be a joy to almost everyone you meet.

8 THURSDAY ☿ *Moon Age Day 25 Moon Sign Leo*

You enjoy a good balance of give and take right now and should find certain individuals to be far more giving than might have been the case only a few days ago. With plenty of determination you won't be easily beaten but there might be one particular issue that despite all your efforts should now be reluctantly abandoned.

9 FRIDAY ☿ *Moon Age Day 26 Moon Sign Virgo*

Organisational issues take up a good deal of your time at the moment. This could be related to work but is just as likely to be concerned with social issues and your need to ring the changes in terms of out-of-work interests. Keep in touch with friends who are at a distance and maybe arrange a long journey to be taken next year.

10 SATURDAY ☿ *Moon Age Day 27 Moon Sign Virgo*

Don't allow yourself to be manipulated by others. Rather, you need to look at all situations yourself and to react according to your own conscience. Aries is a natural leader and not a follower, which is why in the end you can bring others round to your own point of view. It's a fine line though because bullying won't work.

11 SUNDAY ☿ *Moon Age Day 28 Moon Sign Virgo*

A restless streak starts to become evident and ordinary, everyday tasks could be something you will run a mile to avoid. You need a change of scenery and even if you only manage to get an hour or two in your local park it could be enough to make you feel entirely different. Learn to delegate and let others do some of the work.

12 MONDAY *Moon Age Day 29 Moon Sign Libra*

The Moon is now firmly in your opposite zodiac sign and is almost certain to bring stumbling blocks that you will have to work hard to get through or round. It might actually be better not to try too hard, but rather to wait for better trends before committing yourself to anything that requires real effort.

13 TUESDAY *Moon Age Day 0 Moon Sign Libra*

If you struggle to stay on top of things today, you have to ask yourself whether it is even necessary in some cases. There might be certain issues that would be best left to their own devices, whilst you concentrate of matters that are self-evidently important. In any case, your capabilities are going to be much improved tomorrow.

14 WEDNESDAY *Moon Age Day 1 Moon Sign Scorpio*

This is a good day for constructive career building and for planning ahead as far as your professional life is concerned. There could be a slight lull in romantic potential, but that is probably because you are so busy doing other things. Try not to be too selective about jobs and sort out some of the less pleasant ones, too.

15 THURSDAY *Moon Age Day 2 Moon Sign Scorpio*

The social contacts you have been making of late can be of great use to you right now. This will be especially true in professional situations. Don't be too surprised if you are being sought out for special treatment from those in authority and show how pleased you are when someone close to home seeks your opinion, too.

16 FRIDAY *Moon Age Day 3 Moon Sign Scorpio*

If there have been specific worries at the back of your mind, you should discover that at least a few of them now disappear like the morning mist. Maybe you have worried them out of existence, but it is far more likely that you were making too much of an issue of them in the first place. A feeling of significant relief could follow.

17 SATURDAY *Moon Age Day 4 Moon Sign Sagittarius*

The support you now receive from others should be stronger at the moment than has seemed to be the case for quite some time. Make use of this situation by relying on colleagues and good friends, whilst at the same time checking details and making certain that you are still fully in command of all situations yourself.

18 SUNDAY *Moon Age Day 5 Moon Sign Sagittarius*

This is an excellent time to be on the move and the chances of you making some real gains in the material world are extremely good. At the same time, you should remember that this is a Sunday. The year is moving on rapidly towards its end and the weather will hardly be improving. Get some fresh air and enjoy the great outdoors while you can.

19 MONDAY *Moon Age Day 6 Moon Sign Capricorn*

Stand by for a busier time in store, though not particularly for today. Plan ahead, but without pushing yourself too much at the start of this working week. For most Aries people, it will be enough to say what you want in order for others to do their best to see your plans mature. You have some good friends around you now.

20 TUESDAY *Moon Age Day 7 Moon Sign Capricorn*

There is a great deal in your chart now about self-expression, leisure and pleasure. All you need in order to make today go with a real swing is a good dose of optimism, together with the support of like-minded friends. Personal attachments should be strengthening and family members actively seek your advice around now.

21 WEDNESDAY *Moon Age Day 8 Moon Sign Capricorn*

It is important to take life one step at a time and to avoid being overwhelmed if everything seems to be happening at once. Don't bite off more than you can chew at work and when you are at home allow relatives or your partner to do something on your behalf. This isn't the most energetic day of the month for you.

22 THURSDAY *Moon Age Day 9 Moon Sign Aquarius*

Now you begin to show real insight and your independent approach to life is both refreshing and useful. Not everyone seems to have your best interests at heart, but you do have what it takes to turn situations to your advantage, no matter what others might think. You should be dreaming up new and revolutionary ways to do tedious jobs.

23 FRIDAY *Moon Age Day 10 Moon Sign Aquarius*

Emotional confrontations are to be strictly avoided today. There is a distinct possibility that you could get yourself involved in some sort of argument that will be both pointless and potentially destructive. When it comes to issues about which you have no real opinion, make it plain that you are willing to be flexible.

24 SATURDAY *Moon Age Day 11 Moon Sign Pisces*

Social pleasure can now be integrated into your overall plans for the weekend. This is a good time to mix business with pleasure and to get satisfaction from both. You may begin new friendships at this time and also get a positive response from people who are in positions of authority. All in all, a positive period for Aries.

25 SUNDAY *Moon Age Day 12 Moon Sign Pisces*

A few delays are more or less inevitable at the moment and there appears to be little you can do about the situation but wait and see. That might leave you with time on your hands. Since you can easily get restless, right now you need to take on new projects that give your active mind something to think about.

26 MONDAY *Moon Age Day 13 Moon Sign Aries*

Stand by for an explosion of possibilities and do everything you can to meet this very progressive period in a reactive way. The lunar high should bring better general luck, together with a fund of new incentives and plenty of energy to pursue them. All in all this could be the most influential day that you will encounter during October.

27 TUESDAY *Moon Age Day 14 Moon Sign Aries*

This is the best time of the month to be running ahead of the pack. So quick are your thought processes that it is unlikely many people will be able to keep up with you. The new incentives continue and at the same time you have what it takes to sweep someone right off their feet. As a result new romance is possible for some.

28 WEDNESDAY *Moon Age Day 15 Moon Sign Taurus*

Things continue in a very positive way and some situations seem to be turning to your advantage, even without you trying very hard. A combination of past effort and present certainties allows you to glide towards your objectives, whilst on the surface you appear to be the coolest and most collected person around.

29 THURSDAY *Moon Age Day 16 Moon Sign Taurus*

There could be internal relationship matters causing some slight anxiety around now, but this is not created by a powerful or long-lasting astrological trend. For most of the time you are easy-going and find that those with whom you mix during the day are just as relaxed as you are. This could be a good day to ask for a favour.

30 FRIDAY *Moon Age Day 17 Moon Sign Gemini*

You should press on with your daily business, generally unconcerned about issues that are not really yours to sort out. If you get yourself tied down with worries that rightfully belong to other people, you will slow your own progress. It's fine to stand up for your friends, but don't try to live their lives for them.

31 SATURDAY *Moon Age Day 18 Moon Sign Gemini*

It isn't what happens on the surface that really interests you today, but rather the undercurrents of life. For once Aries becomes a deep thinker and your intuition is turned up full. You can do yourself a great deal of good, both personally and professionally, by tuning in to what people are thinking rather than what they are saying.

♈

November

2015

1 SUNDAY *Moon Age Day 19 Moon Sign Cancer*

Today should be good for all matters that involve communication with others. Not only do you know what to say, but you also have a good idea about the best way to approach different sorts of people. Some routine tasks should be passed to others right now, whilst you deal with the most important jobs.

2 MONDAY *Moon Age Day 20 Moon Sign Cancer*

A romantic matter might give you the run-around today, which is why you need to be paying attention and to ignore any sort of goading that appears to be taking place. Stick to what you know and stay cool when provocation is around. You have the patience to win the day easily if you simply take your time.

3 TUESDAY *Moon Age Day 21 Moon Sign Leo*

Intimate encounters should look good today. The closer you are to any given individual, the more willing you should be to spend time in his or her company. Dealing with strangers is likely to be far less appealing and you may prefer to stick to what you know whilst present trends continue.

4 WEDNESDAY *Moon Age Day 22 Moon Sign Leo*

In some situations it appears that others get the upper hand. As long as you play it cool this doesn't really matter. Even matters that look distinctly difficult can be dealt with smoothly if you simply choose the right words. Give yourself time to think about a necessary change of scenery that is on offer.

5 THURSDAY *Moon Age Day 23 Moon Sign Leo*

Finding the best qualities in others is often natural to you, and is an ability that is much enhanced right now. As a result you can increase your own confidence because you know you are getting the support you need. This makes it easier to take a few calculated risks that could mean significant movement in your life.

6 FRIDAY *Moon Age Day 24 Moon Sign Virgo*

There is a chance that some helpful news from faraway places could turn the tide of certain situations at the moment. Getting on with what is necessary can be something of a chore and it is quite possible that you will decide to alter your routines. Not everyone finds this easy to come to terms with, but those you really care about will co-operate.

7 SATURDAY *Moon Age Day 25 Moon Sign Virgo*

Getting on well depends not only on what you do but also on whom you know. That is certainly the case for you today. Comfort and security, whilst they have a part to play in your thinking, are not really all that important right now. You may be climbing personal mountains, and that isn't always easy.

8 SUNDAY *Moon Age Day 26 Moon Sign Libra*

Energy and enthusiasm are low and they won't get too much better for the next couple of days. Before today is out the Moon occupies the zodiac sign of Libra, bringing the lunar low as far as you are concerned. Take life steadily. Enjoy a laugh in the company of friends, but avoid pushing too hard towards any destination.

9 MONDAY *Moon Age Day 27 Moon Sign Libra*

Although you are still quiet and life may not be offering what you would wish early in the day, the lunar low soon passes and you can enjoy a generally happy and even eventful sort of Monday. Get the dross out of the way before lunch and then set out on a journey of self-discovery – but take a friend along.

10 TUESDAY *Moon Age Day 28 Moon Sign Libra*

A sense of general impatience permeates your life today. For a week or more now you have been trying to settle yourself, not an easy process for anyone born under your astrological sign. Little by little you are getting where you want to be, but Rome wasn't built in a day. Aries needs to be both positive and patient.

11 WEDNESDAY *Moon Age Day 29 Moon Sign Scorpio*

Relationships are now boosted by better communications and it's easier to get on with even usually awkward family members. Make the most of positive trends financially and be willing to take a small risk if necessary. Generally speaking this is not an ideal time for solo projects. Co-operation works best.

12 THURSDAY *Moon Age Day 0 Moon Sign Scorpio*

What you hear from others could be of tremendous importance today, so it is worthwhile hanging on to every snippet of gossip that comes your way. Ring the Thursday Moon Age Day changes by getting out of the house at some stage during the day. Of course, if you are committed to work that won't be a problem.

13 FRIDAY *Moon Age Day 1 Moon Sign Sagittarius*

You are likely to find yourself busy and on the go today, whether you like it or not. The chance of a stay-at-home, domestic sort of Friday is unlikely. However, once you have the bit between your teeth you will relish the cut and thrust of everyday life and can really make progress on all fronts.

14 SATURDAY *Moon Age Day 2 Moon Sign Sagittarius*

Domestic matters may find you more involved than has been possible for a week or so. Your mind turns towards the needs that loved ones have of you at present and there is plenty of reason to suspect that most of your spare time is being used to make others feel more secure. Leave a few moments just for yourself.

15 SUNDAY *Moon Age Day 3 Moon Sign Sagittarius*

It looks as though under present trends you will enjoy the company of a wide range of different sorts of people. You show great charm and a willingness to take the other person's point of view on board a little more than would sometimes be the case. If you are at work, look out for new avenues for your existing talents.

16 MONDAY *Moon Age Day 4 Moon Sign Capricorn*

Professional developments should be on a roll today and you have what it takes to make a good impression on just about everyone you meet. Don't be fooled into thinking that someone knows better than you do about any aspect of your life, because you are especially shrewd, calculating and in the know at present.

17 TUESDAY *Moon Age Day 5 Moon Sign Capricorn*

You can glean some profound insights today and show yourself to be very astute and even quite psychic. In a practical sense, you need to dump outmoded concepts or efforts that have proven themselves to be a waste of time. Don't chase rainbows that you know are going to disappear as soon as you approach them.

18 WEDNESDAY *Moon Age Day 6 Moon Sign Aquarius*

Following the same general pattern that has been obvious for a while now, you tend to break ties that are no longer of any use to you and will be making new friendships all the time. The potential for romance is good and especially so for Aries people who are presently forming new attachments or formalising more casual ones.

19 THURSDAY *Moon Age Day 7 Moon Sign Aquarius*

Your inner drive is fully in gear and what you want more than anything at the moment is to feel that you are improving in every possible way. This might lead you to a desire to remodel yourself even more, perhaps through diets or health regimes. If so you need to proceed carefully. You can achieve anything in time, but be steady.

20 FRIDAY *Moon Age Day 8 Moon Sign Pisces*

There could be an intimate issue that is on your mind at the moment and if this is the case you ought to get it sorted out before you move on to other matters. There are some small surprises in store at present and though most of these will work to your advantage you do need to be in a position to respond to situations quickly.

21 SATURDAY *Moon Age Day 9 Moon Sign Pisces*

Dream up something to do that pleases you exclusively. You've done a great deal of thinking and acting on behalf of others during the last couple of weeks and you now deserve a treat yourself. Things are going to get very hectic at the start of next week so also think about taking life steadily on this early winter Saturday.

22 SUNDAY *Moon Age Day 10 Moon Sign Aries*

A combination of factors, including the arrival of the lunar high, puts you firmly in the driving seat of your own life and offers great incentives when it matters the most. Consider yourself to be in the most favoured position of the month and do whatever is necessary to prove how capable you are in the eyes of others.

23 MONDAY *Moon Age Day 11 Moon Sign Aries*

The positive trends are set to continue today and you will be able to start the working week on a very positive note. Niggles from the past can be dealt with in a flash and there could be plenty of opportunities for breaking new ground. Your social instincts look especially good.

24 TUESDAY *Moon Age Day 12 Moon Sign Taurus*

There is now the same powerful desire to get things done that typifies your zodiac sign. The restrictions are out of the way and nothing will hold you back when you are certain of the direction you wish to take. Pay attention to what your partner or a good friend is saying. If you do, you could save yourself a lot of effort.

25 WEDNESDAY *Moon Age Day 13 Moon Sign Taurus*

A desire for personal freedom is now so strong within you that you would do almost anything to avoid feeling fettered. There is nothing at all odd about this as far as you are concerned. The fact is that Aries needs space and can soon get very frustrated and even ill if it is restricted to places or situations that feel constraining.

26 THURSDAY *Moon Age Day 14 Moon Sign Gemini*

This is a fascinating day to be out and about and it should not be spent doing either boring or routine jobs. If your time is your own find some way to get out and about, most rewardingly in the company of someone you love to be with. The evening could offer interesting social possibilities, as well as some new sort of diversion.

27 FRIDAY *Moon Age Day 15 Moon Sign Gemini*

You can apply your intuition to problem-solving today and should have a good deal of fun on the way. There are areas of your life that might need improving, or else things you want to address out there in the world as a whole. Whatever you turn your mind to at present is grist to the mill of your curiosity.

28 SATURDAY *Moon Age Day 16 Moon Sign Cancer*

This is going to be a good day when it comes to problem solving and with regard to personal advancement. Now is the time to let those in positions of authority know how good you are and today could be the focus of new responsibilities. Whatever the demands are you are up for them and should be enjoying life.

29 SUNDAY *Moon Age Day 17 Moon Sign Cancer*

You should be in for a happy phase at home and will be creating an especially caring and sharing sort of environment for yourself and your loved ones. The most pleasing moments you encounter today are likely to come along courtesy of family members and you show yourself to have more time than usual for domestic issues.

30 MONDAY *Moon Age Day 18 Moon Sign Cancer*

It looks as though career issues are going your way and there are possible gains coming in a number of different potential directions. Remove obstacles from your path when it is possible to do so, but also be willing to listen to the advice of someone who is an expert and who does know better than you.

December

2015

1 TUESDAY *Moon Age Day 19 Moon Sign Leo*

This is a day of busy comings and goings. Avoid arguments and direct confrontation, unless you know it is absolutely necessary. Relatives and friends should be rather more co-operative than strangers, some of whom you may tend to mistrust. Some of your natural Aries boldness could be taking a holiday.

2 WEDNESDAY *Moon Age Day 20 Moon Sign Leo*

This is a time when you would really gain from a complete change of direction. Travel of any sort would be good and you need the cut and thrust of everyday life in order to be happy with your lot. Concern for the underdog is strong and the brave qualities of Aries are on display.

3 THURSDAY *Moon Age Day 21 Moon Sign Virgo*

This is a period to be consolidating on recent efforts. Although you might not get quite as much done in a concrete sense as you would wish you can still get ahead. Part of the secret is to allow other people to take some of the strain. This is a particularly good interlude for making contact with friends at a distance.

4 FRIDAY *Moon Age Day 22 Moon Sign Virgo*

There is now a strong emphasis on physical pleasures and on luxury. To others, you appear to be the most entertaining person around and this is a situation that is not likely to change markedly for the next few days. You can afford to push your luck and insist on getting your own way in at least a few respects.

5 SATURDAY *Moon Age Day 23 Moon Sign Libra*

It would be hard to keep ploughing on regardless in the face of the lunar low, but that's probably what you are going to do right now. All the encouragement in the world to rest and wait is likely to fall on deaf ears with Aries now. So if things go pear shaped and you end up fatigued, don't say you were not warned!

6 SUNDAY *Moon Age Day 24 Moon Sign Libra*

You can't expect to make quite the level of practical or professional progress you might wish, but maybe that isn't particularly important to you on a Sunday. Despite the lunar low, you get much from personal attachments and it is towards those you care about the most that your mind is turning at this time of year.

7 MONDAY *Moon Age Day 25 Moon Sign Libra*

It seems as if the main focus is now definitely on communication, probably with all manner of people you haven't had a great deal to do with previously. You know how to have a good time at the moment and will be quite willing to put yourself out to please others. However, it might be sensible to keep a lower profile at work.

8 TUESDAY *Moon Age Day 26 Moon Sign Scorpio*

Whilst concentration regarding detailed tasks may suffer somewhat today you can enjoy personal matters to the full. It's true that not everyone seems to be quite in line with your thinking but you can probably have some fun talking them round. There are signs that an old flame could burn again in your life any time now.

9 WEDNESDAY *Moon Age Day 27 Moon Sign Scorpio*

You may insist on being the team leader today. Although this could put someone's back up a little, it's true that you do have what it takes to head almost any faction. Avoid arguments by installing a second in command, which should keep the most contentious individuals quiet. Avoid intrigue at all cost.

10 THURSDAY *Moon Age Day 28 Moon Sign Sagittarius*

There is likely to be much to discuss today and your powers of communication are especially noteworthy at present. Strong opinions predominate around you, but it's good to know that your own considerations are being taken on board. How could they fail to be? You are an Aries, after all.

11 FRIDAY *Moon Age Day 0 Moon Sign Sagittarius*

You should be a rather good listener today and the sympathy and understanding you show for others marks you out as being very much softer by nature than you sometimes wish to appear. You will even enjoy doing the odd good turn, especially for people you think have recently had a hard time.

12 SATURDAY *Moon Age Day 1 Moon Sign Sagittarius*

You may be even more outgoing and sociable than usual at the moment. The Sun presently occupies a position that is sure to put you at the head of things. At the same time, you relish the company of many different sorts of people, most of whom find you fascinating and good to have around.

13 SUNDAY *Moon Age Day 2 Moon Sign Capricorn*

You tend to be more and more outgoing as the days slip by and will certainly be in the limelight where social situations are concerned. For some reason your popularity is especially high now. It could be that you are presently encountering many different invitations and you will be loath to turn down any of them.

14 MONDAY *Moon Age Day 3 Moon Sign Capricorn*

Today should see a boost to practical affairs that continues to work in your favour. If it seems you are somewhat short of cash, delve deep into your originality and think up new ways to earn more. The upcoming Christmas season now becomes a serious issue in your mind – somewhat belatedly, it might seem.

15 TUESDAY *Moon Age Day 4 Moon Sign Aquarius*

There is much to gain from all co-operative ventures at this time and particularly so in the case of Aries people who are involved in business partnerships. Personal attachments are also well starred. It might be the magic of the season, but you could find you feel deeply romantic and more inclined to speak words of love.

16 WEDNESDAY *Moon Age Day 5 Moon Sign Aquarius*

You now have quicker access to information that can easily be turned to your advantage. If you are involved in some inward battle, for example stopping smoking or trying to control your weight, keep up your efforts, but at the same time avoid being quite as hard on yourself as might sometimes be the case.

17 THURSDAY *Moon Age Day 6 Moon Sign Pisces*

You tend to be slightly more excitable today and could easily be overreacting to situations that would normally not move you much at all. Avoid arguing simply for the sake of doing so and whenever possible take the line of least resistance in discussions. If you shoot from the hip too much you will regret it later.

18 FRIDAY *Moon Age Day 7 Moon Sign Pisces*

With the Moon in your solar twelfth house at the moment it is clear that you become better at expressing sympathy and that your ability to see what makes others tick is more enhanced than usual. Today might be slightly quieter, but if so this is only because you are happy to watch, wait and listen for a few hours.

19 SATURDAY *Moon Age Day 8 Moon Sign Aries*

You can easily get others to see things your way, which could turn out to be one of the most gratifying aspects of this period. Confidence is growing and even if it isn't possible to address the professional or practical aspects of life today it should be clear that at least your prior planning is on course. A good day is on the cards.

20 SUNDAY *Moon Age Day 9 Moon Sign Aries*

Your thinking tends to be inspired and with the lunar high present you can put many of your most important thoughts into action. It's time to get busy and to show everyone who you are and what you are capable of doing. On the way you should encounter more than your fair share of good luck.

21 MONDAY *Moon Age Day 10 Moon Sign Aries*

This could be an ideal time for travel and also for spiritual studies of almost any sort. There is something quite introspective about you right now, though this is a period that will only last for a few days. Talk to as many different sorts of people as proves to be possible today.

22 TUESDAY *Moon Age Day 11 Moon Sign Taurus*

Practical setbacks are possible and when they come along all you can do is to deal with them one at a time. By tomorrow everything should look quite different, which is why it would be sensible to shelve certain jobs until later. If you don't, you could find yourself having to repeat them later in any case.

23 WEDNESDAY *Moon Age Day 12 Moon Sign Taurus*

Although Christmas is generally a time for families and close friendships, Aries has the ability to use the social gatherings in order to further professional objectives. This could certainly be the case today, particularly since your cheerful and happy nature is making a favourable impression on so many potentially influential people.

24 THURSDAY *Moon Age Day 13 Moon Sign Gemini*

It looks as though Christmas Eve is likely to be something of a mixed bag for you, but you do have what it takes to make others sit up and take notice. Your opinions at the moment tend to be rather set and a little more flexibility would help. Present planetary trends make you very committed to family members.

25 FRIDAY *Moon Age Day 14 Moon Sign Gemini*

Christmas Day arrives and is going to bring with it a need for company. In turn, other people are apt to bring out the best in you, so a really intimate, family Christmas seems slightly less than likely. Be on your guard for any chance to break with usual routines and don't be frightened to ring those Christmas changes.

26 SATURDAY *Moon Age Day 15 Moon Sign Cancer*

This is a day during which you need to vent some of your pent-up frustrations. These can probably be dispersed simply by enjoying a change of scenery and by doing something different from the Christmas norm. If the weather is good you might opt for a walk in the country or by the coast. Whatever you choose, variety is essential.

27 SUNDAY *Moon Age Day 16 Moon Sign Cancer*

The way to stay happy today is through social matters and group encounters. Aries needs company right now and relishes the cut and thrust of interesting and stimulating conversation. Not everyone seems to be on your side, but you can easily brush off a few comments that seem custom-made to annoy you.

28 MONDAY *Moon Age Day 17 Moon Sign Leo*

You need more genuine fun and stimulating romance in your life at this time and the planets are likely to oblige. Entertaining others is as simple as encountering them in social situations or inviting them round to your home. Most people find you absolutely fascinating to have around and will be happy to tell you.

29 TUESDAY *Moon Age Day 18 Moon Sign Leo*

Most issues will be going your way, mainly because you are willing to take life by the scruff of the neck and shake it into what you want. There is a slightly ruthless streak about, but as long as you look out for the good of others, as well as feathering your own nest, this shouldn't be much of a problem.

30 WEDNESDAY *Moon Age Day 19 Moon Sign Virgo*

Your tongue and wit are both extremely sharp at present and whilst this is a very positive trend there is just a slight possibility that you could offer someone offence without realising you have done so. Maybe just a little more concern for the sensibilities of people in your vicinity is called for right now.

31 THURSDAY *Moon Age Day 20 Moon Sign Virgo*

Other people will certainly notice the speed with which you express yourself at the moment and more than a few of them want to be involved in your present ideas. Your mind is already well into the New Year and it is unlikely that you will be making too many resolutions. Aries knows what it wants and plans well ahead to get it.

RISING SIGNS FOR ARIES

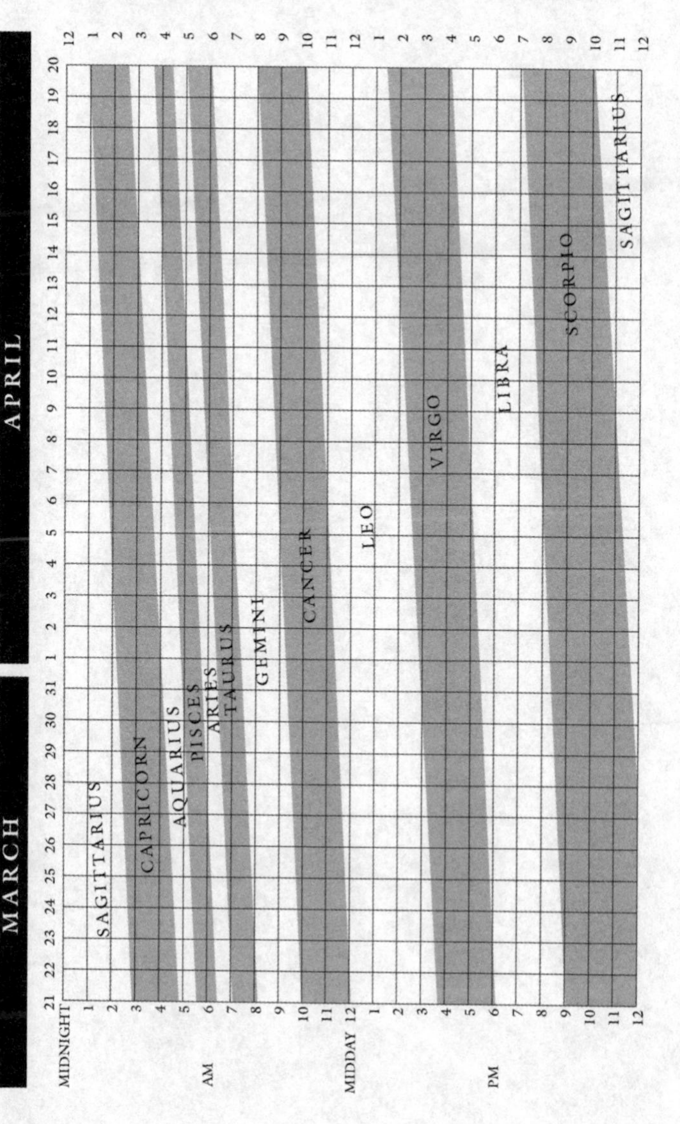

THE ZODIAC, PLANETS AND CORRESPONDENCES

The Earth revolves around the Sun once every calendar year, so when viewed from Earth the Sun appears in a different part of the sky as the year progresses. In astrology, these parts of the sky are divided into the signs of the zodiac and this means that the signs are organised in a circle. The circle begins with Aries and ends with Pisces.

Taking the zodiac sign as a starting point, astrologers then work with all the positions of planets, stars and many other factors to calculate horoscopes and birth charts and tell us what the stars have in store for us.

The table below shows the planets and Elements for each of the signs of the zodiac. Each sign belongs to one of the four Elements: Fire, Air, Earth or Water. Fire signs are creative and enthusiastic; Air signs are mentally active and thoughtful; Earth signs are constructive and practical; Water signs are emotional and have strong feelings.

It also shows the metals and gemstones associated with, or corresponding with, each sign. The correspondence is made when a metal or stone possesses properties that are held in common with a particular sign of the zodiac.

Finally, the table shows the opposite of each star sign – this is the opposite sign in the astrological circle.

Placed	Sign	Symbol	Element	Planet	Metal	Stone	Opposite
1	Aries	Ram	Fire	Mars	Iron	Bloodstone	Libra
2	Taurus	Bull	Earth	Venus	Copper	Sapphire	Scorpio
3	Gemini	Twins	Air	Mercury	Mercury	Tiger's Eye	Sagittarius
4	Cancer	Crab	Water	Moon	Silver	Pearl	Capricorn
5	Leo	Lion	Fire	Sun	Gold	Ruby	Aquarius
6	Virgo	Maiden	Earth	Mercury	Mercury	Sardonyx	Pisces
7	Libra	Scales	Air	Venus	Copper	Sapphire	Aries
8	Scorpio	Scorpion	Water	Pluto	Plutonium	Jasper	Taurus
9	Sagittarius	Archer	Fire	Jupiter	Tin	Topaz	Gemini
10	Capricorn	Goat	Earth	Saturn	Lead	Black Onyx	Cancer
11	Aquarius	Waterbearer	Air	Uranus	Uranium	Amethyst	Leo
12	Pisces	Fishes	Water	Neptune	Tin	Moonstone	Virgo

